COWBRI
BUILDINGS AND
PEOPLE

A selection of the buildings of Cowbridge
and the people who have lived in them

COWBRIDGE RECORD SOCIETY
1999

Contributors

Text: Betty Alden, Jeff Alden, Iris Ashby, Christine Banning, Margaret Chappell, Sue Collier, George Crabb, Jeanne Crabb, Barbara Davies, Margaret Hawkins, Genevieve Haynes, George Haynes, Keith Jones, Betty Lewis, John Meredith, Keith Morgan, Mike Nicholas, David Pierce, Richard Press, Mary Provis, Tony Provis, José Rawlins, Rosemary Ryland, Catherine Thomas, Mary Wallis, Christine Young

Illustrations: Betty Alden, Jeff Alden, George Crabb, Barbara Davies, Ailsa Pierce, Christine Young

Editor: Jeff Alden

Published by
Cowbridge Record Society,
1 Mill Park, Cowbridge, CF71 7BG

Printed by
Keith Brown and Sons Ltd.,
55 Eastgate, Cowbridge

ISBN 0 9537029 0 1

PREFACE

The idea for this book came from a series of classes in local history which I took in Cowbridge for the Department of Continuing Education of Cardiff University in 1998-9. We had originally intended to use census and tithe map information to build up a picture of Cowbridge in the 19th century, but such was the enthusiasm of the class in obtaining deeds, ferreting out documents, enquiring of owners and doing detailed research that the information we obtained extended both backwards and forwards from our stated period.

We realised that some of this research had been done before but the results had remained in the recesses of the researchers' files and were never published; on the other hand, some of the documents we used had apparently never seen the light of day since they were first written. Judging from the interest, not only of members of the classes but of the property owners and others who learned what we were doing, we decided to form the Cowbridge Record Society whose aims were to record the sources of information we found about Cowbridge property, and to publish some of the salient facts about most of the significant buildings in Cowbridge.

In writing this book we have been well aware of the pace of change of use for some buildings: the current land use indicated in this book is that of summer 1999. We have researched nearly all the buildings in High Street, quite a lot in Eastgate, but very few in Westgate - pressure of time and space have set limitations. For those who would like to find out more about the properties (and for many we have much more information than could be published in this book), our sources of information and further details have been listed in our research files, copies of which have been deposited in Cowbridge Library, Bridgend Local Studies Library in Park Street, Glamorgan Record Office in Cardiff, Cardiff Library Local Studies Department, Cardiff University Social Studies Library and the National Library of Wales in Aberystwyth.

We would like to thank all those who kindly made available their property deeds and gave other information, and also the staff of the libraries listed above for their help. Should any readers have additional knowledge, we would be pleased to hear about it - our research is never-ending! We would remind readers that nearly all the buildings described are private properties, and their inclusion in this book does not suggest any rights to visit.

Jeff Alden

CONTENTS

Map . . . . *Inside front cover*

Preface . . . . *Page 3*

Cowbridge: An Introduction *5*

Ribbon Map *10*

THE BUILDINGS

1 High Street to 83 High Street (North side) *12*

Westgate and the Butts *50*

Masons Arms to 2 High Street *56*

The Limes and Eastgate (South side) *85*

Eastgate (North side) *95*

COWBRIDGE: AN INTRODUCTION

For a town of fewer than 5000 people, Cowbridge is remarkably well-known. As a stopping-off place on the A48, especially on 'international days', its pubs have long been popular; before the by-pass was built, its traffic jams were notorious. Its school has produced lawyers and rugby players of distinction (and a poet and actor or two) and the town has in the last 50 years provided two of Glamorgan's cricket captains. Traditionally the market town of the Vale of Glamorgan, its restaurants, wine bars, shops and boutiques now bring in visitors from further afield.

Cowbridge is the only town in the 'old' Glamorgan with a Town Gate still existing - indeed the only town with some of its medieval town walls still standing; it is also the town which has best preserved its late 18th/early 19th century character. Change has come in the past 30 years, but the core of the town with its extension in Eastgate and Westgate still has a lot to show the historian or the interested visitor.

Roman Cowbridge

When the Romans extended their great main road, the Via Julia Maritima, westward from Caerleon towards Neath, they had to cross the Thaw valley. They established a military presence here at Cowbridge, partly as a defensive measure against the local Silures whose Iron Age camp can still be seen on Llanblethian Hill. Roman Cowbridge was possibly called Bomium - the Antonine Itinerary, a 4th century route guide, mentions a fort called Bomium situated between Isca (Caerleon) and Nidum (Neath).

It was only in 1977 that any real evidence of a Roman settlement at Cowbridge came to light; remains of shops and houses were found in the Cooper's Lane excavation opposite Old Hall. Excavations in 1980/1 behind Bear Lane - where Arthur John's car park now stands - exposed the foundations of a large military bathhouse, complete with furnace rooms and hypocausts (and roof tiles stamped with LEG II AUG showing that the Second Augustan Legion of the Roman army used the site). The 'dig' in the Bear Field showed signs of iron-working, and a fine carved stone lion (a funerary monument, now in the National Museum of Wales) was unearthed at the west end of the town in a rescue dig before the Hopyard Meadow flats were built. There was obviously a sizeable military presence here and a civilian settlement too, but when the Second Augustan Legion moved away to defend Hadrian's Wall, the town faded away, buildings crumbled and as far as we know between the 5th and 13th centuries the town ceased to exist. The Roman road however remained; its course can be followed today as the main road through the town, up Primrose Hill and then along the stony track to the top of St Hilary Down.

Cowbridge New Town and the Middle Ages

The Normans entered South Wales at the end of the 11th century and soon established control of the lordship of Glamorgan. The 12th and 13th centuries in Britain were a time when many new towns were created; by the middle of the 13th century the lord of Glamorgan, Richard de Clare, decided that a new town be established along the east-west road at Cowbridge. The first charter of this medieval 'Milton Keynes' was signed on March 13th, 1254. It was called Longa Villa (Long Town) so it seems likely that by then its linear shape had already been established; it soon became a walled town with four gates. The present day town shows considerable evidence of the Norman foundation; the South Gate, some of the town walls, the church and the layout of the gardens in the middle of the town, the long narrow 'burgage plots' (about eight metres wide and 60 metres long), all date from this time. It is also possible that some of the buildings lining the High Street today were originally of medieval origin; for example, the demolition in 1977 of a fairly unprepossessing 18th century building at 75 High Street showed that the facade concealed a substantial 14th century merchant's house.

The new town was established for economic reasons: for the lord to obtain rents and for the tenants to establish markets for trade and to free themselves of duties they would otherwise have to perform. It was a successful venture; the number of burgages increased from 59 in 1262 to 276 in 1306. By this time the town would have expanded well beyond the limits of the walls, along Westgate and Eastgate where the burgage plots provide striking evidence of this medieval expansion, confirmed by excavations of three medieval houses in Hopyard Meadow.

Cowbridge's role in the Middle Ages was as a market town for the surrounding agricultural area; its market place was in the High Street near its junction with Church Street, next to where the Guild Hall then stood. The fortunes of the town and its market fluctuated as did the size of its population, but it was very much an urban settlement with the occupations of its inhabitants ranging from a variety of trades and crafts through to a few professional people and some minor gentry. Many significant buildings remain from this time, the *Bear, Masons Arms* and *Duke of Wellington* public houses, the Great House pharmacy and the Ancient Druid among them. Holy Cross church saw the addition in 1473 of the south aisle, and in 1608 Cowbridge Grammar School was built next to the church by the Stradling family of St Donats. This became the property of Jesus College, Oxford in 1685.

Eighteenth and Nineteenth Centuries

The 18th century was largely a time of prosperity. Fine Georgian town houses, such as Caercady House, Old Hall and Woodstock House were built or rebuilt for the gentry of the Vale, partly because residence in Cowbridge gave the right to vote in parliamentary elections. Cowbridge was also of administrative importance: throughout the century the town played host to the Quarter Sessions, usually held at the *Bear Hotel* during the weeks after Easter - for minor offenders and debtors - and the King's judges came to the town for the more serious cases, held at the Great Sessions at the Guild Hall. Even from the Quarter Sessions people were sentenced to be transported to the colonies, while from the Great Sessions many were condemned to the gallows on Stalling Down. "See Caercady before you die" was a local expression, as condemned prisoners would have been taken from the Cowbridge cells up the Roman road to Stalling Down to glance northwards for the last time towards Caercady House near Welsh St Donats.

During the Sessions most of the important social events of the year were held: horse races, dinners, plays, meetings and balls, at which many of the county families would be present. The Revd John Carne of Nash, a keen observer and participant in the social events, spent £28 at Cowbridge races in 1770, watched and no doubt took part in card-playing sessions at the *Spread Eagle*, and subscribed to a music club which was also held at the *Eagle*.

Trade increased, with some of the produce of the Cowbridge merchants being sent over the Bristol Channel through the port of Aberthaw, and traffic along the main roads was also stimulated. In 1764 a turnpike trust was set up by act of parliament, whereby local landowners were empowered to charge tolls if they reconstructed the road from Cardiff to Swansea. Toll gates were set up at both west and east ends of Cowbridge, as well as outside the South Gate. The narrow and awkward gates in the town walls, which must have proved great obstacles to coach traffic, were removed about this time - Thomas Edmondes of Old Hall obtained permission in 1753 to remove the West Gate which crossed the road at the *Masons Arms*, while the East Gate near the House of Correction was gone by 1775. By contrast the corporation repaired the South Gate in 1805 (and has done so a number of times since).

Up to 1786 mail had been carried by post boys on horseback but after that date the mail coach ran from London to Swansea three times a week. Horses were changed every ten or 12 miles, the *Bear Inn* being the Cowbridge stop at first. This method of travel was not cheap: even though competition reduced prices, advertisements of 1804 show that the cost was 1/- a mile. By this time the *Bear, Spread Eagle, Black Horse* (an earlier name for the *Duke of Wellington*) and the post office were all involved in the hire of post chaises.

The Guild Hall - outside which John Wesley preached in 1743 - stood in the middle of the High Street and was a considerable obstacle to carts and coaches. The Revd John Montgomery Traherne, who planted the trees in the clump on Stalling Down, produced a plan in 1823 for a new Town Hall on the site of the old House of Correction; this was completed in 1830 and the old Guild Hall removed, thereby easing coach traffic through the town but only for 20 years or so. The coach trade faded away about 1850 in face of competition from the South Wales Railway which ran from Cardiff via Llantrisant to Bridgend.

The railway eventually came to Cowbridge - too late and running in the wrong direction! It opened in 1865, running south from Llantrisant and was extended to Aberthaw in 1892. Trade from the agricultural Vale of Glamorgan, however, was never enough to ensure its success (so the Aberthaw section closed in 1930 and the remainder eventually in 1951). Croft Street, Croft Terrace and Aubrey Terrace were built as railway-men's houses. Otherwise only the bridges in Aberthin Road and Cardiff Road and the line of the railway north and south of the town remain as evidence. The station stood where Millfield Drive is today.

There was little Victorian building in the town: The Shield, Graig House and Stafford House are the best examples of Victorian middle-class hous-es, while the Grammar School in Church Street was rebuilt by Jesus College in Gothic style in 1847. As well as the Grammar School there were a number of celebrated private schools, notably the Eagle Academy held in the old *Spread Eagle* inn and a school for young ladies held by the Misses Culverwell in Great House. In addition, a National School was opened in Cardiff Road in 1838, the Board School on Broadway in 1876 and the Girls' High School in 1896.

The Twentieth Century

The development of motor traffic had its effect on Cowbridge, but per-haps less here than in many other places. There was no industrialisation, and it was only with the construction of the by-pass in 1965 that rapid change was initiated - in the building of housing estates around the town, and in the change in character of the shops and businesses.

★ ★ ★ ★ ★

In the following pages we have attempted to show something of the history of a selection of the buildings of Cowbridge, and some details of the people who owned and lived in them. We have followed a route starting at 1 High Street (which is next to the old bridge - opposite Bridge Garage) and have then moved westwards along the north side of High Street (that is, the Town Hall side of the street) up to Woodstock House, No 83. After a brief excursion into Westgate and the Butts, we return along High Street from the *Masons Arms* as far as Church Street, and thereafter from the *Duke of Wellington* along High Street over the bridge to the Limes. Eastgate (the southern side) follows up as far as the Ancient Druid and then St Crispin; our return journey selects some houses on the north side of Eastgate before looking at the continuous stretch of buildings from Kumalo House to the betting shop at No 91.

There are two maps to help the reader - on the inside front cover and on pages 10 and 11.

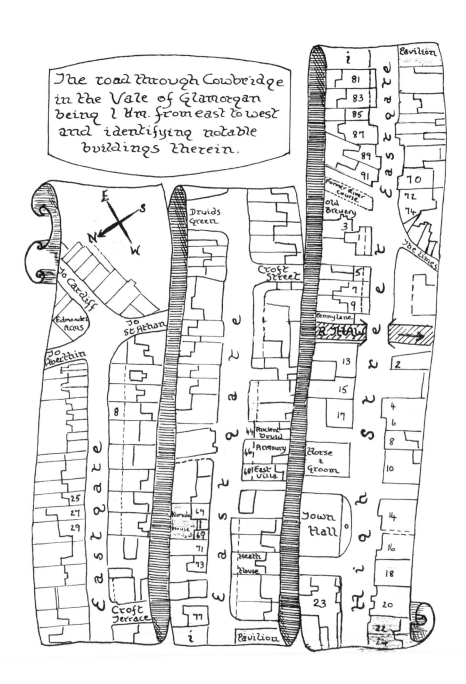

The road through Cowbridge in the Vale of Glamorgan being 1 km. from east to west and identifying notable buildings therein.

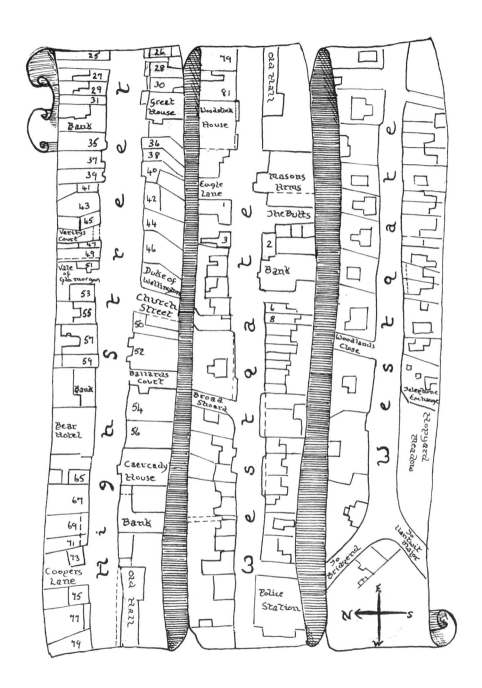

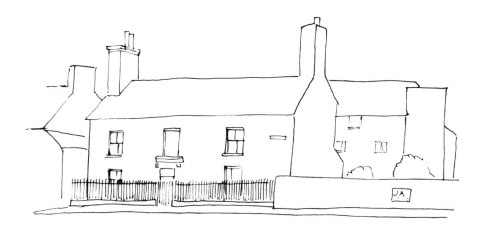

1 and 3 High Street – Glanthaw and The Brewery

Glanthaw and the south wing of the Brewery are grade II listed buildings. A plaque on the wall outside Glanthaw records the reconstruction of the river bridge in 1911; the Thaw used to flow under the road at this point, then after emerging at the entry to the Limes turned at right angles to flow parallel with the main road before going south at today's bridge. Old deeds refer to this area between the current bridge (built in the 1950s) and Glanthaw as 'The Bridge'.

Edward Ballard senior, bailiff and freeman of Cowbridge, purchased a plot of land next to the river and the old bridge in the early 1800s. He developed Bridge House (No 5) and on the eastern part of the site built another house, Glanthaw. This house has had a variety of tenants - including John Chambers in 1828, John Nicholas in 1843, Richard Davis in 1851 - each census recording a different inhabitant. However, the Davies family (originally coming from Somerset to work in the brewery) has lived here for much of the 20th century.

It was Lewis Jenkins of the *Horse and Groom* who developed the brewery. Edward Ballard had built a store house for keeping 'deals and other timber' with an upper storey as a wool loft (he was a skinner and so wool was a by-product of his trade). His son James, an innkeeper, had enlarged and converted it into a malthouse by 1828. It was still a malthouse in 1887 with Jabez Evans as tenant when Jenkins bought the property and set up a brewery. Hansards took over the property in 1900 (when it contained a brewery, malthouse, engine house, caskshed, stable and coach house). It passed to the ownership of Thomas Morgan and Sons and finally closed as a brewery in 1955. It is now a private residence.

5 High Street

The building which we see fronting the street today dates from the early years of the 19th century. The jettied side and rear is older, however. This is part of the building which was described as 'ruinous' in 1809 but which in the latter half of the 18th century was one of Cowbridge's many public houses - the *Royal Oak*. It is tempting to link this to the inn of one William Howard for which a detailed inventory exists, for the unusual layout of the rooms, with a Lower Room and Dark Room, seems to tally, but so far no firm documentary evidence has come to light. Certainly in 1768 the occupier was Thomas Morgan, victualler; the owner was Evan Thomas of St Brides Major. Various Thomases owned the property until after 1800.

Edward Ballard, a skinner and a man of some wealth and importance, bought the plot which included 5 High Street in 1809. He proceeded to develop this site, building not only the 'new' house but also a coachhouse and chandler's shop to the north. It stayed in the Ballard family until 1887, being the family home from about 1850 when Edward Ballard, ironmonger, Thomas Ballard, ironmonger and chandler and Martha Ballard, proprietor of houses (and their nephew Thomas Acton Ballard, maltster) lived here.

For a short period in the 1880s it housed the girls' school of Jane and Annie Llewellyn, who lived here with four boarders aged between seven and 13 in 1881, but then again became a family house, known as Bridge House. Towards the end of the 20th century it was divided into two properties.

7-11 High Street

Nos 7 and 9 are on land which in 1809 was pasture bought by Edward Ballard as part of a larger plot including Nos 1, 3 and 5. He built one house here, which in 1843 and 1851 was occupied by John Stockwood, then a solicitor's clerk, who later moved as a solicitor to Woodstock House.

This substantial house was occupied by a number of wealthy people - in 1861 by Mary Perkins, a landed proprietor, with her sister and her niece, Corina Davies (who later moved to No 55), and in 1871 by Lydia Colton, a twice-widowed annuitant born in Llanblethian. She had first married one of the de Burgh Morgans of Colwinston, and their unmarried daughter Anna lived with her; Anna was here alone in 1891. The house was then replaced by the two houses which we see today. No 7, Sunnyside, was occupied in 1912 by Anne Lewis, the widow of Lewis Jenkins the brewer, and her new husband David, an engine driver; in No 9, Myrtle Villa, was William Williams, a draper's assistant.

We can trace ownership of the Penny Lane site back to a Thomas Morgan, a farmer from Llantrithyd, in 1784; it passed to his nephew Jenkin Morris, a maltster, in 1823, and then to his nephew David Williams. Elizabeth Williams lived here in 1843 and 1851 (with the Spencer brothers from Aberthaw as lodgers), followed in 1861 and 1871 by Mathias James, a stonemason journeyman. Soon after 1880 John Hopkins and Sons, builders and monumental masons, opened their workshop here. It remained a mason's yard until the building of the shopping precinct in the 1970s. John Yeoman, greengrocer, has occupied the High Street site from that time.

13-17 High Street

This was where the *Horse and Groom* was originally situated. The earliest record we have is of 1773, when the owner was Thomas Williams; the publican from 1788 to 1800 was William Richards. In 1875-6 it temporarily suffered a change of name, to the *Horse and Jockey*, and in 1891 moved to its present location.

At the turn of the 19th century, the site of the present Nos 13 and 15 was developed by Richard Watkins, a local master tailor, as one private residence. It overlooked a small watercourse, the Thaw then flowing further to the east. It is suggested that the architect was William Burges, of Castell Coch fame - but none of his flamboyance is evident here!

By 1912, Watkins was still living in No 13 - which had been extended somewhat to the rear - but No 15 housed Charlie Davies the hairdresser and William Stoddart the dental surgeon, while in No 17 was Henry Goulden's grocer's shop. Charlie Davies gained an enviable reputation when the American millionaire, William Randolph Hearst, regularly sent a Rolls Royce to convey him to St Donat's Castle to dress the hair of famous contemporary American filmstars.

No 13 is now occupied by Patterns haberdashery, No 15 by Domus Interiors, and No 17 by Hollwars clothes shop (Ann Talbot's in the 1960s). To this day, Richard Watkins' successors - the Lewis family - reside on the premises, and a daughter runs Patterns.

19 High Street - The Horse and Groom

There was originally a small house and garden here, owned in the late 18th century by Thomas Thomas and in the early 19th by Edward Ballard junior. The present *Horse and Groom* was built in 1891, and is an imposing Victorian structure. Some of the outbuildings remain from the old *Horse and Groom*, which was previously on the adjoining site to the east.

The landlord of the old inn between 1878 and 1891 was Lewis Jenkins, a town councillor (not to be confused with Alderman Lewis Jenkins of the Vale of Glamorgan Brewery) and something of an entrepreneur. He opened the Cowbridge Brewery at 3 High Street in the 1890s. He moved on to lease the *Butchers Arms* opposite, and the *Railway Inn*, but died in 1897.

Samuel Hayter was landlord of the new *Horse and Groom* between 1914 and 1926. He had been brought up in the previous house on the site, and his uncle was Cowbridge's first photographer. Sam was a popular landlord, well-versed in weather lore, and this was a much-frequented venue on market days and fair days. He was also a keen cricketer and played for the town team, being a demon underarm bowler.

Two other families had long links with the *Horse and Groom* in the mid 20th century - the Griffiths and the McNeils: Bert Griffiths (a councillor), then his wife, then Don their son, were followed as licensees by Glyn McNeil (who was mayor in 1959 and 1966) and his wife. The layout of the inn then, with the public bar on the right and the saloon bar on the left, was different from today's open plan.

Town Hall

The Guild Hall of Cowbridge stood, until 1830, in the middle of the street near the *Duke of Wellington*. It had long been an impediment to traffic along the main road, so when the opportunity came to convert the town's House of Correction into a new Town Hall, it was willingly seized.

An act of parliament was passed in 1576, giving permission for a prison or Bridewell in Cowbridge, but the first reference to the House of Correction on this site was in 1725. In 1805 it was rebuilt (using stone from Thomas Wyndham's quarry near the West Gate, lime from Stalling Down, Pennant stone for floor slabs and Bangor slates for roofing). By 1829, however, a large new prison was built in Swansea, and so the site became available. Revd J M Traherne of St Hilary had by then had plans drawn up, so the conversion, rapidly completed under the supervision of Isaiah Verity, used the basic structure of the House of Correction. Thus the cells remain, now housing the town museum; one, set out to resemble an original cell, gives a good idea of its squalor and lack of space.

The cupola, housing a new clock - the old one had not worked well after its transfer from the original Guild Hall - was built in 1836 as a gift of the Bishop of Llandaff, Dr Edward Coplestone, who then lived at Llandough Castle. Alongside the Town Hall was the shambles with its butchers' stalls, and walls blocked off both sides of what is now Town Hall Square. In 1895, the Town Hall was enlarged (filling in the open sides at the rear); in 1902 the Fire Brigade headquarters were established in what is now the Lesser Hall and kitchen, and remained here until the second world war.

23 High Street - Taynton House

This house and the pump at the side are both grade II listed buildings.

The Tayntons were among the *crachach* of Cowbridge in the 18th and 19th centuries. Nathaniel (1693-1754) lived here, as did his son Francis (1731-1794) a founder freemason in Cowbridge, a minister of Holy Cross church and an active member of the Court of Common Council. Details of Nathaniel's will and subsequent tax assessments suggest that his house occupied two-thirds of the present frontage, but the western part, previously the *Black Horse* and before that Mary Ralph's, was purchased in 1768. The *Black Horse* continued as a separate establishment until 1813, but from then on all of Taynton House became the family home. The last Taynton to live here was the Revd Francis, who had been a curate in six Vale of Glamorgan parishes and who died in 1870.

The house became the home of Ebenezer Miles, a local solicitor who was one of a number of liberal-minded businessmen of Cowbridge, helping to start half-day closing for employees. The solicitor's practice was later taken over by Wayne Morgan, and then by Mr Walker (of Gaskell and Walker). The front part of the building is now used by The Travel House, Jenny Wren jewellers and Raggs dress shop; Off the Beeton Track restaurant, Cowbridge Electrical Services and a number of houses occupy the remainder of the plot.

The electrical shop was originally stables, taken over in 1895 by Gibbs and Brown the printers. After they moved to Eastgate, Henry Gibbs the baker took over and baked bread here until after 1945.

25 High Street

This was one of the many properties of the Carne family of Nash Manor (and of Great House, Cowbridge).

In 1682 it was leased to a Mary Tanner after the death of her husband Thomas, and while subsequent occupants are known to include John Reed, Ann Tanner, John Lewis and Thomas David, research has shown little of interest until the building was recorded as a public house, the *Three Boars' Heads*, in 1827. There are earlier records of a *Three Boars' Heads* existing since 1795, but without a specific location, so we can only suggest it was here in the intervening period. After that, however, it remained as a public house until after 1926, tenanted mainly by the Howells in the 19th century. Some Cowbridge residents remember the last licensees, the Upshalls, who supplemented their income with some pig farming.

When the licence ended, J J Ryan the saddler took over - a skilled workman, he could set his hand to all sorts of leather goods. Estate agents and stationers have been more recent occupants.

The mounting block at the front of the building, grade II listed, is of 18th or 19th century origin, and would have been useful for customers of either the *Three Boars' Heads* or the public house at No 27.

27 High Street

This is a grade II listed 17th century building which was owned by the Edmondes family from at least 1743 until 1922 when it was sold to Edwin Villis. It has a crux beam roof construction and under the slate roof are the remains of the earlier thatch. The inner front wall of the upstairs room is daub and wattle and the two windows in the gable end were retained when the building was refurbished. In the shop premises there are two fine old exposed beams, together with a stone vaulted chamber in the rear of the shop. An archaeological excavation showed that the building was erected on the site of an earlier medieval house; the extension to the rear was made on the site of the stables. There is a passage between No 27 and No 25 leading to North Road.

The fame of this building must however lie in the fact that as an inn it went under five different names! The earliest records show that the house was occupied by William Jenkins, a weaver, in 1697, but Howell John, an innkeeper, was there in 1707. The inn was named as the *Lower White Hart* in 1733 when David John, a saddler, was also the publican. The name was changed to the *Red Lion* in 1744 (publican, William Evan in 1759, and Richard Lougher in 1782). However, it was the *White Hart* by 1793, the *Hope and Anchor* between 1820 and 1825, and by 1826 had changed again to the *White Lion*, which name was to have been found at an earlier date on the south side of the High Street. It remained as the *White Lion* until the 1920s, having a large number of landlords during that time.

Since then it has been a greengrocers and a cake shop, and now a dress shop (Lois) has been in business for many years.

29 High Street

This is a 17th century property, which was extended to a second floor and to the rear of the building in 1912. In the garden there was a two-storey bakehouse which was demolished in the middle of the 20th century. The house and shop were probably built on the foundations of an earlier building, and at about the same time as the adjoining properties on the east and west.

In 1697 it was described as 'of Pierce Deere', a wealthy shopkeeper and alderman, and remained in his family at least until 1730. The house was certainly owned by the Carnes in 1730, and then leased to David John the saddler and occupied by members of his family; it remained Carne property until it was bought by William Lewis in 1875. For over 100 years it was a grocer's shop, in the early part of the 19th century run by James Hiscock followed by John and Margaret Gibbon, and by 1871 William Lewis, a farmer and grocer, and his wife Margaret. During the next ten years Morgan James had married William's daughter Jennet and they were running the shop. By 1891 Morgan Thomas, who was a baker and a grocer, and his wife Mary, Jennet's younger sister, had taken over the business, moving to 33 High Street after 1914.

Sometime after 1914 Mr Escott had a butcher's shop here, which later moved to the south side of the High Street, and Mrs Escott ran a fried fish shop; by 1934 the shop premises were occupied by Arthur Sanders, bootmakers and repairs, and today it continues as a family-run shoe shop.

31 High Street

It is likely that this 17th century property was owned by Evan Seys in 1730, occupied then (and in 1750) by the interestingly named Sampson Sweeting of Aberthin. Robert Cooke was taxed on the house in 1773 and by 1815 it was the home of Thomas Hunt, yeoman, and his wife Mary. After her death in 1827, Thomas Howell, a baker, the son of Thomas Howell a shoemaker from Aberthin, inherited the premises. Thomas Howell had a baker's shop here and this was continued when Thomas Williams and his wife Mary took over the business, which they purchased in 1862, and continued until around the end of the century. It then became a grocers run by David Williams, and in 1926 Arthur Sanders had a boot repair business here. Later, it was a private house and for a few years the front window became an additional display area for the adjoining shoeshop. From 1995 it has been Glyn Jenkins' delicatessen.

The two windows on the first floor gable end date from the 18th century. It was quite a substantial property and had a number of buildings at the rear, including a malthouse which had been converted into a schoolroom by 1821 and used as such until at least 1862, by which time there was also a bakehouse. The malthouse/schoolroom is where the newly refurbished cottages are today.

It has been said that when Mary Williams was running the business at the end of the 19th century a travelling circus, Bostock and Wombwell's Menagerie, was passing through Cowbridge and that Mary gave the elephant a bun. Many years later when the circus was travelling through again, the elephant tried to enter the shop to help itself to a bun - an elephant never forgets!

33 High Street - Lloyds Bank

No 33, a much altered building - the fibre-glass pillars are but the latest in a long line of changes - has records of its ownership dating back to the 1770s. Then it was owned and occupied by Robert Taynton and his wife Elizabeth. Robert was for 38 years a naval lieutenant; his memorial plaque in Holy Cross church describes him as "an affectionate husband, a kind relation, a sincere friend, and to him the poor and indigent never applied in vain". After his death, the property passed to his niece Elizabeth, and her husband Benjamin Sykes, from Bristol, though they did not live here.

John Parsons, from Dorset, and his Wiltshire-born wife Sarah had arrived in Cowbridge by 1841, and soon acquired the house. From 1848 it was their grocer's shop; they did well enough to employ two men by 1861. John was also an agent for fire and life insurance. After he died in 1880, he was succeeded in the business by his son Thomas, who played the organ in the Wesleyan chapel, had a pipe organ here in his home and was a keen natural historian. At the back of the building was Norton's timber store and carpentry business.

In 1907, the shop transferred to David Williams and Son, grocers from Bridgend, and was managed by the building's residents, the Millmans, until the 1950s when it was sold to Lloyds Bank. During the 1970s, the eastern part was used for a while as the Gas Board showroom and the town's post office.

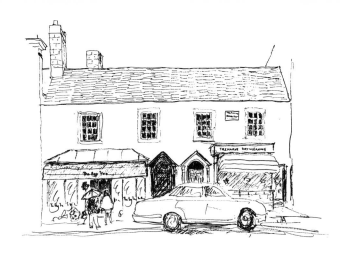

35 High Street

This - together with No 37 - is a grade II listed building, largely because of the panelled doors with fanlights and pedimented doorcases, which lead to the flats above the shops. In the early 18th century this was one of the properties owned by the Seys family. It passed, with many others, to Robert Jones (a relative) towards the end of the century, and was occupied by various members of the Thomas family (Benjamin, then Diana and then Thomas Thomas by 1815).

John Kayes, a Cowbridge alderman, owned the property in 1830, followed by his nephew William Davies. It housed the Thomas family's chemists shop through the middle of the 19th century - Morgan Thomas being followed by John Thomas ('master druggist, employing one man') - before Joseph Rogers, an ironmonger and predominantly a stationer, moved in around 1871. He had four children, and his wife Sarah continued the stationery business after his death in 1882.

Margaret Davies, a widow from Welsh St Donats, lived here for a short time in the 1890s, but by 1895 the house was taken over by John David, auctioneer and estate agent, borough treasurer and registrar of births and deaths. He was a founder of the firm of John David, Watts and Morgan. The Andrews family ran their shop here for over 30 years from the 1930s, selling children's toys and cycles, radios and televisions (S P Andrews), before it was taken over by the present occupiers - Treharne Drycleaning - in 1974.

37 High Street

With No 35, this is a grade II listed building, and was one property until the 1840s. The early history of No 37 is summarised under 35 High Street.

The 1830 owner, John Kayes, was a currier (his business being at 44 High Street) and alderman known as 'tun-bellied Kayes' and was a celebrated figure in the town. In 1819, according to David Jones of Wallington, 11 of the largest men in Cowbridge, Kayes being the biggest, got inside a hollow elm tree at the back of Llwynhelig farm; a wager depended on them drinking much beer while there, and then getting out again - all of which was accomplished. Kayes, who usually had to walk with two sticks, also had his arm broken when thrown out of his carriage against the turn-pike gate in 1828.

His nephew, William Davies, first lived in the property, but on inheriting it after his uncle's death he rented it to Edward Ballard between 1843 and 1861. Ballard's death in that year saw John Kayes Davies as the occupant until 1866, then the building became part of the shops and workshop of the drapery empire of Samuel David Evans next door at No 39. Internal doors provided a link between the two properties. The Evans family ran the business until 1926 when Barry Co-operative Society took over the building as a grocer's shop. Today it houses the Bay Tree florists.

39 High Street

No 39, a grade II listed building, still contains internal 17th century beams and a fireplace, with an unusual inner courtyard. In the 18th century it was occupied by Thomas Thomas, a skinner, and is one of the properties covenanted to pay 12/- yearly for bread for the poor on Sundays. Through the first half of the 19th century, Edward Ballard, skinner, wool merchant and tallow chandler, ran his business here (conveniently sited near the Church Street slaughter house).

From 1843, a draper's business was established by a George Waugh Toogood: he was from Somerset, and employed four assistants and five tailors. Benjamin Williams from Middlesex succeeded him in 1858 and expanded the business. In the 1870s it was run by Samuel David Evans (who from 1857 had Cloth Hall at 50 High Street). He - and later his son Frederick - ran the Vale of Glamorgan Emporium until about 1926, expanding through to No 37 next door, employing many staff and using the grey cloth from Llanblethian woollen mill. Interestingly, Samuel and his wife, both born in Cardigan, employed many people from West Wales as domestic servants. Their other sons became notable Cowbridge businessmen.

After use by the Barry Co-op in the 1930s, the ground floor of the property was taken over by Ivor Treharne for his stockroom and sales of agricultural implements and feeds. From the 1970s it housed Walters Pet and Garden Store until the 90s, since when it has been known as Xantippe, selling French painted furniture.

41 High Street

Of 17th century origin and a grade II listed building, this property contains several noteworthy architectural features, including its 18th century doorway with a fine moulded hood. Early records show that in 1717 it was occupied by the Aubrey sisters. Cecil Aubrey had parted from her husband Edward Portrey of Tyle House, Boverton and their lands had been divided. Between 1765 and 1784, Philip Walton, clockmaker - one of his grandfather clocks is in the collection of the Museum of Welsh Life at St Fagans - lived here, then his son John, a surgeon.

Throughout much of the 19th century, it was the house of John Bevan, Cowbridge solicitor and landed proprietor, who remained single and fought hard for better education within the town. He endowed scholarships to the Grammar School and helped to establish the Girls' High School (occupied by Cowbridge School's VIth form centre today). He died in Varese, Italy where he had lived for many years, and so had let this house to the Prichard ladies, Decima Prichard being the daughter of the vicar of Llangan.

In the early 20th century, it remained a private house, Ty Hen, surrounded by shops. It was then developed for commercial use - as the Easons' butcher's shop, Mrs Hill's grocers (with the Labour Exchange upstairs), the Southgate Restaurant and then a Chinese takeaway. Andrews and Courie pharmacy (with windows from a Charles Rennie Mackintosh design) followed about 1980. Peter Andrews went on to set up Llanerch vineyard to the north of Cowbridge. Lloyds pharmacy now occupies the ground floor, with Elle dress agency above.

43 High Street

This grade II listed building of 17th century origin, with its gable end wall to the street, extends a considerable distance away from the road. Inside, it has massive ceiling beams and 18th century style fireplaces.

A benefactions board in Holy Cross church records Mrs Mary Morgan's house near the Market Place being charged 12/- a year for distribution in bread to the poor of the town, by the churchwardens every Sunday after service. This - 43 High Street - was Mary Morgan's house, occupied by her at least from 1784 to 1809, and owned by her from 1809 to 1824. At that time, the market was held in the middle of the High Street next to the Guild Hall.

Thomas Llewellyn of Verlands House was the next owner, and from the 1840s the Davises, father and son, booksellers, stationers and printers, lived here. David Davis published a number of fine engravings of scenes in the local area; Ebenezer, his son, produced 11 editions of a monthly magazine. Otherwise their products were similar to those of many a small town printer. Ebenezer was the secretary of the Cowbridge Eisteddfod in the 1870s, but in 1885 he, his wife Elizabeth and eight daughters left Cowbridge and emigrated to the USA.

David Brown the printer lived here for a short time, but from 1906 the building was used as an ironmonger's shop and agricultural merchants - for Rees Morgan and Co for a year, and then from 1907 for Arthur John - a family business which continues today.

45 High Street

At the beginning of this century, this 18th century house was a substantial three-storey building which was reduced to two storeys at about the time of the first world war. The adjoining entrance to the attractive Verity's Court preserves its cobbles and protective stones. It was a Seys property, in the ownership of Robert Jones of Fonmon from 1784 until the beginning of the 19th century, then changing to Isaiah Verity and later to Abraham Verity. William Verity had a linen and woollen drapery business here in 1830 and was later joined by Cecilia Verity, who was the occupant in the 1843 tithe returns. She moved from here into Verity's Court and then to Eastgate.

By 1848 it had become a grocery shop which was to remain through to the 1960s. It was started by William Williams and by 1860/61 had been taken over by Philip Griffiths, continued after his death by his daughter Jane. *("P. Griffiths, agent for Dunmore's celebrated Cambridge sausages and pies, Gilbeys wines and spirits, Huntley and Palmer's biscuits, Crosse and Blackwell's manufactures. A trial of his 1/8d tea is solicited. Orders promptly attended to and delivered in the Country weekly.")* Philip Griffiths came from Merthyr Tydfil. He married Isabella Randall, an accountant's daughter, and they had three children, Jane, Ada and Louise. Isabella died soon after he moved to No 45 and he remarried. His new wife Jane died in 1884: Philip died in 1910.

The shop subsequently became Thomas and Evans Ltd, then Peglers, both grocers. It is now the Kitchen Shop, a part of Arthur John's.

47 High Street

This is an 18th century building with grade II listing to the extensions at the rear, two of which have mansard roofs. These were first known as Princes Buildings in 1851 and by 1861 as Verity's Court. The shop front is late 19th century. It had been owned by Isaiah Verity from around 1815 and then by Abraham Verity, a surgeon, in 1830. (Even earlier it was a Seys property - subsequent owners were Robert Jones in the late 18th century, and Charles Vachell, a druggist, before 1815.)

From at least 1830 Joyce Morgan ran a grocer's shop here. She was followed by the sisters Elizabeth and Marianne Morris, stationers and book sellers, who had a circulating library and a 'Berlin Repository'. In the mid 19th century, occupants were Thomas Williams a shoemaker and then William Williams a draper. The draper's business was continued by William Price (with wife, two children and two servants) in 1881. It then became an ironmongers belonging to Evan Thomas. From 1900 Alfred George James, a cabinet maker, had a furnishers and china shop here - he had moved from Eastgate to High Street. He remained here for about 20 years and was followed by Boyles and Co, bootmakers. The property was bought by Thomas John in 1949 and today is an Arthur John shop specialising in outdoor clothing.

49 High Street

The owners of this property have all been members of families linked to the Dunraven or Wyndham estates from at least 1742, when a house on this site was occupied by Richard Bates, until 1913 when it was bought by William Lewis Jenkins. Members of the Bates family lived here for much of the 18th century - including Dr Richard Bates, doctor to Cowbridge School at a guinea a visit. This building may have once extended further west, especially as that was also a Wyndham/Bates building.

In 1815 the property was referred to as a house and shop occupied by Mr Ballard, and in 1830 it was occupied by Edward Ballard junior, an iron-monger, by 1844 being his warehouse. William Lewis Jenkins, the son of Lewis Jenkins of the next-door brewery (and who became a JP, and mayor in 1917 and 1918) bought the property at auction in 1913, having occupied it since 1900. He manufactured and bottled aerated water and lemonade, sealing the bottle necks with marbles. The green glass bottles embossed with the word *Cymedroldeb* (Temperance) can still be seen from time to time in Cowbridge. The bottling store was behind the shop where wines, spirits and bottled ales and stout were sold.

The plot was bought by Arthur John in 1924, and for many years the building was used as a storehouse. This has now been replaced by an arcade leading to a courtyard near the Wool Barn. The front part is occu-pied by Robert E Lloyd opticians, and the rear by Shape hairdressers.

51 and 53 High Street

These 18th century properties have been linked for much of their history, and in 1773 were one property owned by Edward Bates. In 1784 it was the *Greyhound Inn* with Nathaniel Young as the licensee. The Bates family continued as owners until at least 1830 but by 1843 the owner was William Jenkins.

The *Greyhound* continued here until in 1865 the name was used for an inn in Westgate; these premises subsequently became the Vale of Glamorgan Brewery owned by Lewis Jenkins. The malthouse was in what is now called the Wool Barn, with the cart shed and stables for six horses across Bear Lane. Lewis Jenkins, originally from Llantrisant, was actively involved in Cowbridge life. He was an alderman and was made a freeman of the borough in 1923. He and his family lived here for many years before moving to Graig House in Eastgate; he died in 1929 aged 94.

In 1915 the property was leased to William Hancock, brewers of Cardiff, and sold to them in 1923. No 51 was used as the off licence and distribution centre for beers, and No 53 became a private residence. In the 1920/30s Tom David lived in No 53; he was a skilled thatcher and thatched Y Bwthyn Bach, the cottage presented to the then Princesses Elizabeth and Margaret by the people of Wales.

By the 1960s, No 53 was the *Vale of Glamorgan* public house and No 51 the off-licence. The front of No 51 is now Gail Armytage's florists shop, with the rear and first floor the kitchen and hotel accommodation of the pub.

55 High Street

The property of the Talbots of Hensol for most of the 18th century, this was Cissil Morgan's house in 1773; by 1784 it was occupied by Edward Ballard senior, as it was in 1799 when it was sold to John Thomas, a Cowbridge lawyer, who lived at No 57.

By 1843 it was one of a number of Edward Bradley properties and occupied by the Revd John Powell, rector of Llanharry. In 1851 Richard Felton, tailor, draper and postmaster, occupied No 55 with his wife and five children, moving by 1861 to No 59 having exchanged houses with the May family. Joseph May was a groom and ostler but was rather more influential than might be expected; there was a May family pew in the church. Joseph eventually moved on to the *Ancient Druid* at 44 Eastgate; his daughter Margaret married Lewis Jenkins the maltster and brewer.

For much of the rest of the 19th century No 55 was the home of Miss Corina Davies, a well-connected lady from St Athan. In 1900 the property was known as Cambrian House and was the home of William Lewis Jenkins, wine and spirit merchant and 'aerated water manufacturer' - the son of Margaret May and Lewis Jenkins of the Vale of Glamorgan Brewery next door.

Its change of use to shops in the 1960s brought in Headquarters hair salon, Eleganza hat shop and then a health food store. It currently houses a travel agent (Culver Travel) and an estate agent (Watts and Morgan).

57 High Street

No 57 was a substantial property, even being described in deeds of 1850 as 'Great House'. It had been taxed on 20 windows in 1773 when it was owned and occupied by Mrs Cecil Thomas - this is 'Mrs Cecil Thomas's house on the market place' charged with the yearly sum of 12/- to supply bread for the poor. In 1809, her daughter Mary married Edward Powell, a local lawyer, by special licence in the drawing room upstairs.

Edward Bradley, a distant relative, owned the property in 1843 and it was occupied then by Christopher Bassett. In the 1851 census the house was occupied by Mary Anne Thomas, and named The Cross after the preaching cross in the street outside. (The naming of the next-door property as The Cross is recent). Unoccupied in 1861, by 1871 it was the home of the Rich family, James Rich being an Inland Revenue officer from Lancashire.

From 1873 through to the 1920s it was the draper's shop, known as Cloth Hall, of David Thomas and family, and from the 1930s for over 30 years, it operated as Tilley's drapers and outfitters. Mrs Tilley had learned her millinery trade as an assistant to John Williams at 91 Eastgate. During the 1960s it was fondly known as the shop still selling clothing from the 40s and 50s!

In 1970 it was demolished and rebuilt as the Finefare supermarket and later it became the Spar shop, one of the first Cowbridge shops with Sunday opening, even though initially many foodstuffs had to be covered over to prevent sales on a Sunday. I S Wood's dental surgery is upstairs.

59 High Street

The earliest available records of No 59 date from 1773 when Margery Deere occupied a sizeable house here. By 1786 the Revd Evan Jones was owner and occupier, and he remained owner of the property until after 1843. In 1850 it was bought by John Samuel. Throughout the 19th century it housed a variety of tenants, who included Joseph May from Pyle, an ostler, with wife and six children in 1851, Richard Felton, tailor and postmaster in 1861, with two boarders, and Edward Evans, a gardener from Pendoylan with wife, three sons and five male lodgers, all scholars, aged between ten and 21 - presumably attending the Grammar School - in 1871.

Surprisingly for such a large and probably valuable property, 1881 saw the family of an agricultural labourer, Thomas David, living here (admittedly seven people in all) and 1891 that of a general labourer, Thomas Jenkins.

In 1894, the building was conveyed to the Metropolitan Bank of England and Wales, and it was about this time that the present building was erected: it was known as Oakley House. Robert Thomas, from a farming family of Barry and Moulton, was the manager; the bank office fronted on to the High Street while the manager and family lived in the rest of the house. In 1924, Robert Thomas, while remaining manager of the bank, bought the property from the Metropolitan Bank which moved into the adjoining premises. His son, Herbert R Thomas, developed the business of chartered surveyors, auctioneers, valuers and estate agents here, where it remains today.

61 High Street - HSBC Bank

No 61 was very nearly the site of the original Cowbridge School. A deed of 1667 identifies it as the house of Edward Stradling called the Prior's Tower. We know that Sir Edward Stradling, the founder of the Grammar School, had intended to establish the school in this tower, but Sir John Stradling decided to build it in Church Street. The history of this site, however, goes back much further. An excavation in 1981 uncovered medieval remains - and showed that the North Gate of Cowbridge existed at the far end of the garden. (Roman pottery from the 3rd and 4th centuries was also found.)

Tax assessments of the late 18th century show that this was a substantial house, occupied by Dr Edward Bates, a prominent Cowbridge citizen. The owners were all linked with Penllyn Castle - Lady Vernon, Mrs Gwinnett, Lord Clarendon, and later the Homfrays.

A watchmaker, Samuel Marks, operated here in the early 19th century, then for a short time it became the National Provincial Bank, its manager being Samuel Hornsby from Jamaica. By 1861 the bank had moved to Westgate, and for the rest of the 19th century this was the home of Thomas Felton and family. The son of Richard (in No 59), he was a chemist, druggist and dentist, as well as the town's postmaster after his father, so the building acted as a post office as well as a chemist's shop. Leeches, 3d each, were kept in a glass jar in his shop window.

Later, the property housed Morgans the butchers until it was sold to the Midland Bank in 1919, and rebuilt in 1923 (architects Woolfall and Eccles).

The Bear Hotel

This grade II listed building was originally a hall-house of late medieval date, the layout of rooms on the ground floor facing the street preserving the original pattern. Noteworthy features inside the building include a mantelpiece with a carved leopard (visible behind the lounge bar), another part of a medieval fireplace in the reception hall, a 16th century doorway and fireplace in the small lounge bar, 16th century beams over the lounge bar, and a 17th century plaster ceiling over the small lounge. To the north, the upstairs meeting room and the downstairs barrel-vaulted 'Bear Pit' excite some architectural historians: this part is also medieval but was formerly separate from the house. The upstairs was converted into an assembly room in the 18th century when the bowed end was added; this is probably the part which was registered in 1738 for Quaker meetings.

Formerly the Cowbridge town house of Llanmihangel Place, it has long been linked with the Thomas, Edwin, Wyndham and Dunraven families. A lease of 1667 to John Carne makes no mention of an inn, but the *Bear Inn* is named in 1738. In 1768, Lady Charlotte Edwin leased it as an inn to John Edmondes ('formerly in occupation of Robert Thomas and then of John Giddings innkeeper'); ten years later, when the lease was transferred, it was described 'with stable, long room, cellar and garden'.

For most of its time as an inn, the *Bear* was also an important centre for meetings and balls, only rivalled for a while by the *Spread Eagle*. A meeting here saw the foundation of the Glamorgan Agricultural Society - and indeed many other organisations. The diary of the Revd F W Edmondes records in 1889 "The Nortons had a dance at the *Bear*. The ladies inspected the arrivals from the bow window (of Old Hall)". Earlier, a hunt ball in

1853 saw an outbreak of typhoid, caused by the pollution of the *Bear*'s water supply (waste in the town ditch, just outside the north walls of the *Bear*, had percolated into the groundwater of the well).

From the late 18th century to the mid 19th century, the *Bear* was an important coaching stop on the route between London and Swansea or Milford Haven, providing accommodation for travellers and stabling for horses. There is a well-known story of a runaway coach: when the coachman and guard alighted at Ewenny, the horses continued with the coach and made their own way to Cowbridge. The passengers knew nothing of the problem until the horses drew up at the *Bear;* the guard, however, who had chased the coach on foot, died a few months later.

Among the best-known of the 'coaching' innkeepers were Walter Williams, Christopher Bradley (1785-1804), Michael Glover (who faced competition from Bradley after the latter had left the *Bear* and set up in rivalry at the post office), James Simpson and James Ballard (1824-44). These were all men of some importance in the town, often being sizeable landowners; their successor, too, John Thomas from Ewenny, farmed 50 acres as well as running the inn. He was followed by Mary Ormandy from Gloucestershire, and then her daughter Elizabeth.

It was Thomas Thomas of St Hilary (Tom the Bear), who ran it from 1875 to 1906 - and who then retired to live at Ty Hen at 41 High Street - who designated the *Bear* as an hotel. Other well-known landlords have included Fred Williams (whose son Evan won the Grand National on 'Royal Mail' in 1937) and Geoffrey Evans of Penllyn, the *Western Mail* cartoonist.

65 High Street

In the 17th century, the buildings on this site were owned by the Stradling family of St Donat's, but by the 18th century ownership had passed to the Talbots of Hensol, and then by 1830 to Lord Dynevor.

In 1842, Thomas Matthews, a saddler from Carmarthenshire, married Margaret Lewis, bonnet maker, in Holy Cross church. They lived in No 65 with their young family, but Margaret died early and Thomas's sister raised the two little girls, Judith and Isabella. By 1870, Judith had married William Yorwerth, also a saddler, and they carried on the business here. Of their four children, Thomas (born 1871) continued living here through to the early 20th century.

In addition to being a saddler and harness maker, Thomas Yorwerth was a long-serving town councillor, being six times mayor, and was in 1940 made an honorary freeman of Cowbridge. He was also deputy registrar and the secretary of the Vale of Glamorgan Agricultural Society, important to this farming community. In 1911, he entered into a partnership with Arthur John the ironmonger to buy a number of properties, and later went into partnership with Herbert Thomas as auctioneers. His daughter Judith married Arthur S Evans of the Bridge Garage in 1922, and about this time No 65 became known as Yorwerth and Thomas auctioneers.

It was subsequently Mrs Hinton's paper and stationery shop; since the 1960s it has been a dress shop, estate agents and Mr Ray Davies's bicycle shop before becoming Hedley Davies, men's outfitters, in the 1980s.

67 High Street - Sorrento

This was a substantial three-storey property, with an imposing pillared porch, which was only removed when the building was altered in 1964. In 1773, it was occupied by John Cole, whose son attended the Grammar School and went on to Jesus College, Oxford; he was a fellow of the college from 1818 to 1830. The owner of the house in the late 18th century was Revd Francis Taynton, and the Taynton family continued to own the property into the 19th century.

In 1824, Mary Lewis and her three sons were joint owners, but by 1831 one of the sons - Thomas, an ironmonger - owned the property and lived here with his mother. After they moved, medical men dominated the pattern of residence in the house - Edward Williams, a doctor from Caerphilly, from 1843 to the 1850s, John Phillips, a Somerset-born surgeon in 1871, and George Reynolds a surgeon from Ireland in 1881. Albert Wilberforce Shepherd, physician and surgeon, bought the house by auction in 1895 to be followed by Dr R H S Torney, who named the house Sorrento, and then Dr D J Evans of Woodstock House and Dr John of Bridgend took it over in 1926.

The only exception to medical occupancy noted in the censuses was in 1861, when John Thomas, an auctioneer, livery and stable keeper and a farmer of 42 acres, lived here with his wife, mother-in-law and sister-in-law. Perhaps it is no wonder that he did not stay here long! Much more recently, the Revd Gilbert Thomas, the much-loved vicar of Bonvilston and a noted hymnologist, lived in the house in the 1940s. It is now a soft-furnishing business selling fabrics, china and furniture.

69 High Street

There are not many houses which can claim to being the one-time home of a peruke maker, but in 1765, John Thomas, peruke (or periwig) maker of Cowbridge, who was also a landowner owning properties in Gibbet's Hill and in Westgate, lived in the property on this site. By 1773, it was owned and occupied by a Robert Copin, but strangely in 1784, though Robert still owned the property, it was occupied by 'Robert Copin's wife'. Marital disagreements or not, by 1788 she was his widow, and in 1800 Mary Copin was the owner-occupier.

Early in the 19th century, the house passed into the hands of the Llewellyn family, initially Thomas and then his widow Ann. They were quite considerable landowners, owning the *Bush Inn* and surrounding property. In the 1851 census, Ann aged 78 was the head of the household. She had been born in Cowbridge and was described as an annuitant, maltster and grocer; she had three of her 'children' living with her - John Llewellyn, a medical practitioner, William, the vicar of Penllyn, and Eliza, described as a 'grocer's assistant'. By 1861, however, Ann had died and Eliza, now a landed proprietor, was the head of the household, which included John, their sister Matilda, a niece and a servant. John seems to have taken over in 1871; by 1881 the only Llewellyn left in the house was the 75-year-old William who was still the vicar of Penllyn.

The house was unoccupied in 1891, but other residents included Mrs Alexander in 1912 and the Webbs in 1923. The current use is for Huddarts restaurant.

71 High Street - Prospect House

Long known as 'Mary Shelcott's house' in the 18th century (though who Mary Shelcott, or Gilcot, was we do not know), this was part of the Pierce Cornish estate and was sold on the bankruptcy of John Wilson, Cornish's heir. Mary Gilcot continued as tenant for some years, but by 1784 the owner was Nathaniel Williams and the occupier Anthony Thomas. Mrs Francis Taynton owned the house in 1800, when it was occupied by the Revd J J Jones. By 1815, Thomas Llewellyn owned and occupied the property, but its condition deteriorated so that by 1830 it was taxed as a stable.

It remained in the hands of the Llewellyn family for some time, as the 1843 occupant, Elizabeth Simpkins, was a Llewellyn by birth. Elizabeth lived here (as a fundholder, aged 70) in 1851 with her sister, Mary Llewellyn, and after Elizabeth's death Mary (a funded and landed propri-etor) continued to live here in 1861. Their relative prosperity suggests that the house was rebuilt some time between 1830 and 1843.

The 1871 census saw it unoccupied, but in 1881 it housed John Davies, a retired farmer who had been born in Cowbridge, with his two daughters, both school governesses, two boarders and a servant. Sydney Gibson, an auctioneer and surveyor, originally from Birmingham, succeeded the Davieses, and S D Evans the tailor came to live here in retirement by 1912.

In its transition to commercial premises it was 'Louise - the Gown Shop' between 1967 and 1972. It is now occupied by David Birt, estate agents.

73 and 75 High Street and Cooper's Lane

When a bulldozer 'collided' with the almost derelict corn stores at 75 High Street in 1977, it showed that a substantial medieval building lay behind the 18th century facade (and that in turn had been built over Roman remains).

In the early 18th century, the lane probably housed the tanyard of Thomas Wyndham, with the bakehouse of Richard David adjoining; by the middle of the 18th century, the area had been purchased by Thomas Edmondes and housed two malthouses (Edmondes frequently stipulated in leases of inns that malt should be purchased from these malthouses).

Thus it is not surprising that the courtyard was known as Malthouse Lane, and in the 19th century it contained four or five cottages largely occupied by labourers or journeymen. It is only for No 73 that we can with any degree of certainty work out the names of the inhabitants (Mary Lutton in 1851, James Eddolls in 1861, Elizabeth Morris in 1871, Hannah Britton in 1881 and Sarah Ward in 1891). By 1912, however, one celebrated resident in the lane was 'Jim The Cooper', James Lewis, who made barrels and lived on the premises. After his death, Eddie John used the front, substantial part of the premises as a corn store.

Today, No 73 is a private residence and No 75 houses the Yorkshire Building Society, while the new houses in the now Cooper's Lane are among the few new buildings in Cowbridge to have been well received in the new 'Pevsner' of Glamorgan.

77 High Street

Garden excavations have shown there were buildings on this site in Roman and medieval times. The remains of a 200-year-old stable yard were also discovered; this may well have been used by the 1843 occupant, an ostler named Joseph May, who later became the landlord of the *Ancient Druid* in Eastgate.

It is believed that the present grade II listed building, with its simple two-storey design, traditional windows and small porch, was put up around 1850, and was given the name Tydfil. For the rest of the 19th century it became the home of the widow and children of a blacksmith, John Harman, who had died in the 1840s when the family were living in Westgate. His daughter Susanna, a milliner, remained unmarried and stayed in the house until her death.

At the turn of the century John David, a prominent citizen of the town, took up residence. He was at various times auctioneer, borough treasurer and deputy registrar, and he was a founder member of the firm of auctioneers and estate agents still occupying premises next door but one at 81 High Street. There is evidence that the house was improved at this time. A fine tiled floor was laid in the hallway, holly trees were planted on either side of the front door and the name of the house was appropriately altered to Llwyn Celyn (Holly Bush). Although the house has always remained a private home, Irene Morgan's nursery school was held here in the 1950s.

79 High Street

In 1773 the house was owned by Joseph Kayes, one of a family whose members were known for their broad girth. By 1784 it belonged to John Owen but was rented by several members of the large Reynolds family, many of whom were tailors.

The first of these was James Reynolds who was here with his wife Margaret from 1788 to 1798, the arrival of their fifth child probably causing them to move (they later had three more daughters). They were followed by Samuel Reynolds, probably a brother of James, then another brother, John Reynolds, who lived here with his family until about 1805.

At this time there was a change of ownership to Catherine Williams, the daughter of the Revd Thomas Williams. There was also a new tenant - James Reynolds, son of the first James Reynolds, who returned to live in his childhood home, with his wife Mary. He also was a tailor. They had moved next door to No 81 by 1815 and were succeeded as tenants by William Lewis until 1819, and then by William Williams.

In 1817 the house was acquired by Rees Williams, who owned it until 1874.

Between 1824 and 1831, the tenants were James James and then John Elliot - variously described as a grocer, tea dealer and teaman - who ran his business here. In 1831 the occupant was Lewis Morgan. Henry Johnson, born in Worcester, was here by 1851. He was a watch- and clock-maker (specialising in long case clocks) and later also a jeweller. He lived here with his son and his unmarried sister, Rebecca, a dressmaker, but by 1861 they had moved to 20 High Street.

By 1871 Richard Pickard, born in Trowbridge, Wiltshire, had arrived here with his family from Canton in Cardiff, and opened a greengrocer's shop. They remained here until 1880, when they moved to 40 High Street. By 1881, the house was occupied by the Methodist minister, David Jones, and his wife Anne. When he died a few years later, she established a grocer's shop, run by D H Davies from 1912 until at least 1934. It remained a grocer's (with a sleeping cat in the window) until the next owner, Mrs Caines, died in 1975.

For four years it was a television repair shop before it became Becki's, beginning life as a ladies' shoe shop and now as a fashion boutique.

81 High Street

Prior to 1761 this grade II listed house was owned by David and Ann Jones, and then by Jenkin Howell. When he died in 1766, he left it to his wife Jane and in 1775 their daughter, Elizabeth, inherited. The following year Elizabeth married John Morris of Llanblethian, who was probably a farmer, and the couple lived in the house until he died in 1804, Elizabeth staying on until 1813 and retaining ownership until 1820. She died, aged 96, in 1823 having given the house to her son, Jenkin Morris.

In 1815 James Reynolds, a tailor, was the tenant with his first wife, Mary, having moved from No 79. They stayed here until 1820, during which time the first two of their nine children were born. When the Reynolds family left, Jenkin Morris moved in until he was succeeded in 1828, as owner and occupier, by Thomas Morris. The latter was still living here in 1843, but the owner by then was Edward Davies.

By 1851, the occupier was James Turner, a hairdresser, born in Hereford, and when he died in about 1866, his widow turned their home into a lodging house. She had three lodgers here in 1871, the youngest being 12 and the oldest 72.

Matilda Morson took up occupation later in the 1870s. She was the widow of the Revd James Colin Francis Morson who had been headmaster of Cowbridge Grammar School from 1870 to 1875, when he had died aged 32. It is said that during his period as headmaster the school reached the pinnacle of its success with 26 boys gaining entrance to Oxford. A window in the chancel wall of Holy Cross church is dedicated to his memory. Matilda and her three children stayed in No 81 until at least 1891.

By 1910, the house was occupied by John Arthur Stockwood. He was a solicitor in Cowbridge, as were his father and his grandfather, both also named John. When John Arthur moved in, his grandfather was still living next door in Woodstock House.

William and Nellie Pickard had previously lived across the road at 56 High Street and came to live at No 81 around 1920 with their daughter and son-in-law, Harold Trotman, who later became head brewer at the Pontyclun Brewery. The front two rooms on the ground floor were used as the offices of David and Watts, the auctioneers, where William worked as the managing clerk. He was a town councillor but this did not stop him berating the town council for wasting money, especially in the articles called 'Cowbridge Siftings' which he wrote under the pen-name 'Velox' for many years in the *Glamorgan Gazette*. The articles were often very funny; his pet hate was the Town Hall pump which, he claimed, was never working when he needed water.

William Pickard died in 1937 and Nellie in 1963, aged 96. The Trotmans continued to live at No 81 until Mrs Trotman died in 1970. From that date, the firm of John David, Watts and Morgan took over the whole building where their business of auctioneers and estate agents is still carried on today.

83 High Street - Woodstock House

Woodstock House is a grade II listed building which was bordered on the west by the town wall. The earliest known records show it was the property of the Wyndham family, later to become earls of Dunraven. John Wyndham, sergeant-at-law (the senior law officer in the county) occupied the house in the closing decades of the 17th century. In 1748 his son Thomas was castigated in court - 'for not raising the wall by the West Gate'. He must have been pleased when his neighbour Thomas Edmondes demolished the gate in 1753. During the life of Thomas Wyndham's son Charles, the family changed its name to Edwin: they owned the mansion until the end of the century but by 1759 it was leased to Thomas Williams and in 1800 to the Revd John Nicholl.

The house changed hands several times during the next 40 years. In the 1850s it was occupied by Charles Sylvester and in the 60s by William Haines, both surgeons. John Stockwood, solicitor and town clerk, lived here during the last 30 years of the century, presumably giving the name Woodstock to the house. He was followed at the turn of the century by Dr Richard Moynan, medical officer of health to the borough council; then Dr David Evans (grandson of S D Evans at No 39) bought the house and lived in it from 1921 to 1941. He also succeeded Dr Moynan as medical officer of health as well as being physician for Crossways Orthopaedic Hospital and medical officer to RAF Llandow.

From early on in the war, Woodstock House housed the Food Office and the Maternity and Child Health Clinic providing orange juice, cod liver oil and powdered milk. The clinic - in a front room - closed in the late 1960s. After the war Eddie John of the Eagle Agricultural Stores lived in the rest of the house. It has since been converted into flats.

1 and 3 Westgate - the Spread Eagle

It is heartening to see that after years of neglect, the ballroom or assembly room of this grade II listed building is being carefully restored and refurbished. Perhaps it will play as important a role in the life of Cowbridge as it did in the 18th century, when the Revd John Carne recorded the dances, travelling plays, assemblies and card-playing that occurred here. The room has a fine arched ceiling and four small minstrel galleries; it did also have one fireplace surrounded by Bristol Delft tiles, but they have now been lost. Under the ballroom is the former brewhouse of the inn, also being restored.

The *Spread Eagle* existed as an inn in 1752 when Thomas Edmondes, the then owner, was in dispute with the landlord of the *Bear Inn*; in 1759 it was described as 'recently erected on land purchased from Margaret David, Jennet Bates and others' - but this could well relate to a rebuild of the roadside part of the property. A number of 18th century documents refer to the building as an inn, but the date of its demise is as hazy as is the date of the inception of the Eagle Academy.

This school acquired a fine reputation among the private schools of Glamorgan in the 19th century. John Sterling remembered it as "that comparatively humble academy which supplied the best knowledge of reading, writing and arithmetic to be attained in that remote neighbourhood. The long desks covered from end to end with those painted masterpieces, the Life of Robinson Crusoe, the Hunting of Chevy-Chase, the History of Jack the Giant-Killer, and all the little eager faces and trembling hands bent over these...in that crowded schoolroom the week before the Christmas holidays".

Among the schoolmasters were Thomas Rhys or Reece "in his drab breeches and white stockings" in 1810, John Eliot in 1843, William Lewis in 1851 and another William Lewis between 1861 and 1874. Closure occurred because of the untimely death of Lewis and competition from the newly opened Board School in Broadway.

By 1891, this had become the home of Edward John, and it also became the Eagle Stores, an agricultural implements shop; the ballroom later became a storeroom for wool bales. Today the front of the building is used for Scallywags children's clothes, Cowbridge Balti House (part of the restaurant occupying the arched cellar of the former inn) and Ballantynes, wine importers.

6 and 8 Westgate

In the mid 18th century one building stood on the site of these two houses, and behind it was a barn, orchard and a large garden which had been converted into a bowling green. In 1757 the owner, Robert Lougher, a wig maker, had obtained a mortgage for the property from Thomas Edmondes, and - as frequently happened - was constrained to sell it by 1766 to John Edmondes. It was soon sold on to Walter Williams of the *Bear*.

Early in the 19th century, the house and garden (part in the 'occupation of the overseers of the poor' and part occupied by Thomas Llewellyn, who owned the premises to the east) were sold to John Thomas, the Cowbridge carrier. He erected two houses - one with stable, coach house and large garden for himself, and a smaller cottage. Thomas Llewellyn, by then living in Verlands House, bought them in 1856, but by 1899 they had been knocked down and rebuilt as part of the adjoining terrace.

In 1856, John Thomas still lived in what was to be No 6, and Samuel Howells, a farmer, and his son Samuel, a brewer, in No 8. A varied group of people lived in No 6 during the rest of the century, including Catherine Harris, an unmarried lady from Neath described somewhat mysteriously as 'a seminary', the Joseph sisters who were dressmakers, and Walter Pinfold, a solicitor's clerk. In 1861, the younger Howells with his widowed mother was in No 8, followed by Richard Thomas, though by 1891 Morgan Morgan, a shoemaker, lived here. On the purchase of the buildings by Robert Lane of St Hilary in 1899, the new No 6 was occupied by Sidney Lane, a gardener, and No 8 by Morgan. Both were still here in 1912.

4 Westgate - NatWest Bank

In the 17th century this plot of land contained a mansion and garden, and belonged to the Wyndham family. John Wyndham leased it to Jenkin Thomas of Cowbridge in 1677, but its connection with the Llewellyn family started in 1724 when it was taken over by Jane Llewellyn.

The mansion called The Croft had been replaced by a coach house and two stables by 1813. They were then occupied by Thomas Llewellyn, who within the next six years had built a malthouse, probably to serve the adjoining *Bush* and *Globe* inns, on the site of the coach house.

Deeds of 1856 suggest that the malthouse was still in existence then, but by 1861 the National Provincial Bank had replaced it, having moved from 61 High Street with its manager, the Jamaica-born Samuel Hornsby. The bank did not purchase the property from the Llewellyns until 1870, however. By this time there had been a change of manager - Thomas Payne from Merioneth lived here with his Cowbridge-born wife, and eventually six children, until at least 1891.

Initially the bank had no porch; this was added before 1891. The street frontage was impressive, with railings and stone pillars (two of which remain today), and paving slabs on the pavement which contrasted with the cobbles in front of the *Bush Inn* next door.

2 Westgate

This was the *Bush Inn*. The first innkeeper here - in the 1840s, in property belonging to Ann Llewellyn - was Miles Morgan from St Nicholas. He married Mary Evans of Llantrisant in 1837, and by 1851 they are recorded as having five children. In 1861 Miles is shown as being a victualler and haulier with one of his sons working as a maltster journeyman. The Glamorgan Rate Book for 1874 shows that Miles Morgan also rented a malthouse in Eagle Lane from Revd Thomas Edmondes, and that the *Bush* was then owned by Thomas Llewellyn.

After Miles Morgan's death in 1876, the public house was taken over by Isaac Williams from Llanmaes - like many publicans he had other employment, as a blacksmith. John Kibblewhite from Highworth in Wiltshire had taken charge by 1891 (and by this time the building was owned by the Revd T L Lister of Newport, son-in-law of Ann Llewellyn and the son of Lister the chemist), and then William Hayter and his wife Mary took over in 1897. When William died in 1906, Mary became licensee and she continued here until her death in 1919.

In a 1920 directory, the keeper is listed as Mrs L A Morgan, who later moved across the street to be licensee of the *Pelican* from 1923. In 1923 the licensee of the *Bush* was Mrs Fanny Walker, but after that date it appears to have reverted to a private house.

The Butts

These are without doubt the oldest council houses in Cowbridge! They existed in 1756 and a deed of 1787 acknowledges the corporation's receipt of rent for 'the five cottages by Pwll y Butts, three whereof are now annexed of the workhouse'. The workhouse did not stay long at this spot, for in 1813 four cottages here were leased to Thomas Rhys, the Eagle Academy schoolmaster; at that time the cottages were occupied by Evan Lewis, John Bowen, Margaret David (though a year earlier she had had notice to quit for 'continuing to take in bastard children') and Cecil Jones.

By 1851, there were three cottages occupied - by Richard Rees, a stone mason, David John, also a stonemason, and John Davies, a carpenter. By 1861, however, the house nearest to the main road had become the *Globe Inn*, run by William Llewellyn, while the other two properties housed Matthew Williams, toll collector, and Morgan Davies, a carpenter.

Mary Phillips was the landlady in 1871 and 1881. The inn seemed to expand to take over the cottages, so that by 1891 when Henry Trott was the landlord he had a family of wife and four children plus 15 lodgers living here. The corporation's sanitation report was not favourable! The licensee was fined on a number of occasions for permitting drunkenness on the premises, and so the licence was ended in 1894. By 1897 the building was in a poor state, with the thatched roof falling in on the bedroom ceilings; it was renovated (as three cottages) and then for a short time became a lodging house. In 1912, the residents were Thomas Eddowes (or Eddolls) in the former *Globe*, Elizabeth Lawrence in No 2 and Arthur Lawrence in No 3.

The Masons Arms

The present-day lounge bar and public bar of the *Masons Arms* occupy what was the hall of this medieval house (grade II listed). The trefoil headed window facing on to the pavement, and the stone doorway leading to the pool room are medieval features; the bay window on the front and the fireplace (with wooden lintel over) between the rooms were built in the 17th century. Behind the left-hand room is an 18th century brewhouse. This is architecturally one of the most important historic buildings of Cowbridge, especially considering that the house was built on to the medieval town walls, adjacent to the West Gate, even incorporating them as part of the wall of the public bar. It may well have been linked with the Gatehouse - before the West Gate was removed by Thomas Edmondes of Old Hall in 1753.

However, it has proved difficult to find many old documents linked with the *Masons Arms*. It is possible that Margaret Lougher occupied it in 1773; by 1784 Anne Painter was the owner and William Thomas the tenant. From then it has had a variety of owners and tenants. It seems to have been a desirable licence to hold, as at least two tenants moved here from other public houses in the 19th century (in 1871, the Devon-born Joseph Braddick had moved here from the *Railway Inn*, and in 1881 Thomas Evans, originally from St Lythans, had moved from the *Pelican* across the road). From 1851 to 1865, William Harvey plied his trade of omnibus proprietor, as well as victualler, from the *Masons Arms*.

Ownership passed to Lewis Jenkins of the Vale of Glamorgan Brewery in 1889, and then in 1919 when James Cross was tenant (to be followed by his son Frank) to the Ely Brewery Company. It is now a free house.

Old Hall

The Adult Education Centre contains enough architectural features for it to be classed as a grade II listed building - notably the large 17th century fireplace upstairs, a small window of similar date, and the remains of the classical front facing the garden. Outside, the late 13th century Town Walls enclose the garden on the south and west, with a walkway on the west part leading to a circular bastion.

It is probable that in the 17th century there were a number of houses on the site, with - earlier - the rear of today's garden having been a cunninger or rabbit warren. By the mid 18th century the Edmondes family had added a suite of rooms with a classical frontage and Venetian windows on the garden side to form a substantial house. In an inventory of 1762 we find a library, hall and two parlours, a well-equipped kitchen and brewhouse, and ten bedrooms (but only three of which could be considered to be elaborately furnished, the remainder being for the children or the servants). Of interest in the two lobbies were two orange trees in tubs, and a sedan or bath chair - signs of affluence. There were lots of maps, prints and pictures on the walls, curtains on the windows of the main rooms, and enough good furniture and china to show that this was the home of a family which was comfortably well-off.

For much of the 18th and 19th centuries the western side of the building was used as a separate house - occupied for example in the 1770s by Margaret Gamage and her sister, Mary Carne. By the 1840s the Revd Thomas Edmondes, vicar of Llanblethian, moved into the main part of the property. As a squire-parson (he owned buildings and land in Cowbridge and Llanblethian and coal-mining interests in the valleys), he played a significant part in the social and administrative life of Cowbridge throughout the century. He and his wife entertained frequently and lavishly - details of the menus and guest lists for some of their dinner parties can still be consulted. Croquet on the lawn (where the lily pond is today) and tennis (on the courts where the library now stands) were popular diversions; the stables (where the flats are today) housed the horses, gigs and hansom which were used both for recreation and daily transport. Five children were brought up here, the females marrying well and the males rising to important positions in late 19th century South Wales (Frederick became archdeacon of Llandaff, Charles principal of St David's College, Lampeter and Francis an army officer).

After the death of the Revd Thomas Edmondes came the combining of the two properties and a rebuilding of the street frontage in a heavy 'Tudor' style, with a new stone porch and north-west gable. Internally a new study and billiard room were created. The Edmondes family continued to live in Old Hall until the late 1920s, when came a major change.

The Grammar School, expanding in numbers, needed more classrooms, and so some classes moved into Old Hall in 1932, without making many modifications to the building. The magnificent white-painted library remained (as did the nursery-wall paintings in one classroom), and also a fireplace reputedly carved by Grinling Gibbons. The stables were used to house the headmaster's car, and to store props for the school play; the grass tennis court was used for impromptu games of football. These appear to have been idyllic times - but they came to an end when the building was declared unsafe in 1964.

It proved impossible to save the classical extension - but the ground floor walls and pattern of rooms remain; Glamorgan County Council refurbished the part facing High Street and also had the library and health centre built in the grounds. These buildings, designed by students of the Welsh School of Architecture under the leadership of a local man, John Roberts, are praised in the new 'Pevsner' of Glamorgan. The gardens are a pleasing amenity for Cowbridge, as is Old Hall itself - now used for adult education classes and an art gallery.

62 High Street - Barclays Bank

Intermittently in the 18th and 19th centuries, these premises were an inn and malthouse known as the *Green Dragon*. In 1764 they were leased by Earl Talbot of Hensol to John Giddings, innkeeper of Cowbridge, and then in 1803, sub-leased to Christopher Bradley of the *Bear*. In 1812 the building reverted to a house and shops, being leased by Edward Bates, the then owner, to Moses Godfrey a silversmith and to Elizabeth Bradley. Joseph Lister's druggist's shop was here in 1827.

In the mid 19th century the property was run by John Woods of Cardiff as a spirit vaults for a time but then reverted to the *Green Dragon* in 1858. In 1861 it was no longer an inn, but two private houses, occupied by Georgiana Morgan, a landed proprietor from Carmarthen, and George Rees, a Cowbridge schoolmaster. Charlotte Alexander ran the vaults in the western part in 1868, and in 1872, when Daniel Owen of Ash Hall, Ystradowen bought the property, part was the *Green Dragon* occupied by Thomas Thomas and part occupied by W J Goddard, a solicitor, as a private house.

This is the last record of the existence of the *Green Dragon*, for in 1873 the house (the eastern part) was occupied by the London and Provincial Bank, and by 1881 the bank manager lived on the premises. Thomas Hambly from Clifton (in 1881), James Thomas from Pontypridd (1891) and George Codd (1912) are among the managers recorded. The London and Provincial Bank was absorbed by Barclays Bank, and the property was conveyed to Barclays in 1928.

58 High Street - Caercady House

The present house of Georgian appearance is a grade II listed building. The imposing facade of three storeys includes ground and first floor windows with shouldered architraves, all set around an elegant Doric porch. Originally stables were attached at the side of the property (where High Street Garage is today).

This was the town house of Caercady, near Welsh St Donat's. Edward Jenkin, in 1773 is the first recorded owner; he and his sister had a reputation as being 'neighbours from hell', apparently driving one neighbour to an early grave, and on one occasion heaping a pile of manure in front of the next-door windows!

John Thomas of Caercady, and then his widow Mary Ann Thomas owned the house until the 1870s; John Fraunceis Griffith of Llansannor Court bought it in 1879. Occupants included George Morgan - a watchmaker - in 1843, Michael Farrar, science master at the Grammar School, his family, three grammar school boarders and two servants in 1851 (presumably because the school was being rebuilt), and Mary Ann Thomas herself between 1861 and 1875.

Dr Charles Booth Meller established his surgery here from the 1880s. Such were his medical skills and popularity that he was reputed to have more patients on his register than any rural doctor in Wales. His first mode of transport was a gig pulled by a stallion, with his groom in attendance; dressed in top hat and frock coat, with his beard to his waist, his appearance was most striking. His wife and daughter were both doctors; the latter continues to reside at Caercady House and so it has been occupied by the Meller family for over 100 years.

56 High Street

The first recorded owner of the building was John Roberts in 1756. At that time it consisted of a house with outbuildings, including a stable and brewhouse, at the rear. Access to these was via a passageway between Nos 52 and 54. Roberts was succeeded by his son, also John, who passed the house to his daughter Ann Roberts, who never married.

John Roberts was an apothecary and so the house was used to sell medicines. Afterwards, it became a doctor's surgery, and then a boarding house. The most unusual use was in the 1850s and 60s when it was the stamp office for Cowbridge. In those days, excise stamps were required for the sale of a number of items, including dice and playing cards, medicines and newspapers. The occupier, Eliza Thomas, also sold jewellery and china and for many years ran a lodging house here.

For the first half of the 20th century, the building was the West End Garage, repairing and servicing vehicles and housing the agencies for Austin, Daimler and Morris-Oxford. It also handled motor bikes. During the second world war it was used to store fire engines.

The building's owners have included Dr William Salmon who moved here in 1803. Originating from a wealthy Suffolk family, he had been the sole trustee of a trust which was disputed in court over many years and led to his ruin. He left Suffolk and came here to work as a doctor, first at Cottrell Park and then in Cowbridge.

His son, also a doctor and also William, visited the site of the Battle of Waterloo so soon after the fighting had finished that many of the dead had not yet been buried. He was a military surgeon, and although not there officially he stayed to treat the sick and wounded. Young William was more fortunate than his father. He married Hester Thomas Deere, the heiress to the Penllyn Estates, and when he died in 1896 he was a rich man, owning around 350 acres of land. Aged 107 when he died, he is believed to be both the longest living doctor and freemason in the world. He also outlived six of his seven children.

William inherited No 56 from his father and in 1845 gave it to his daughter, Rosa, in trust at the time of her marriage to Stephen Spranger, the son of a rear admiral. The ownership via the Salmon–Spranger Trust lasted three generations. For all that time, the principal trustee was William Rees Mogg, a Somerset solicitor whose family had originated in Wick. The name survives today, as the solicitor's great grandson is Lord William Rees-Mogg, the author and journalist, formerly the editor of *The Times* and deputy chairman of the BBC.

Between 1896 and 1912, the building was owned by John Fraunceis Griffith. He lived in Llansannor where in 1884 his home was the first in Glamorgan to be fitted with electric light. Griffith's tenant at No 56 was William Pickard. He was managing clerk at David and Watts, auctioneers, and also a part-time journalist. Around 1920 he lived across the road at 81 High Street.

In 1912, Annie Jones acquired the premises for her husband 'Billy' Jones to run a garage. It was sold in 1967 to the Manning family from Bridgend who continued to operate the garage until 1976 when it was purchased by Mr and Mrs Eddershaw. They converted it to a furniture and toy shop on three floors, and since 1980 it has been Chamberlains, selling furnishings and decorative items.

54 High Street

This is a grade II listed building. Although combined with No 52 as a large house with a coach house in the 18th century, it became a residential property, one of a number owned by Isaiah Verity, soon after 1800.

The first tenants then were the Godfrey family who lived here for more than 40 years, Moses Godfrey being a maker of long case clocks, with white enamelled dials. In 1851 and 1861 Eliza Thomas, jeweller, lodging house keeper and stamp distributor lived here - only to move next door to No 56 before the next census. John Henry Davies was here in 1871 with wife and daughters (two of whom were schoolmistresses) and four scholars, and this was a school for a short time. From 1873, however, William J Davies "embosser on glass, writer, grainer, decorator, house and sign painter, paper-hanger etc" lived in the house through to the early 20th century.

Some Cowbridge residents still remember Miss Goulden's confectioner's shop here; others would be surprised to know that the ground floor housed part of the West End Garage in the 1960s. The change to Farthings wine bar and restaurant occurred in the 1970s.

The buildings towards the rear of the property were originally some of the Ballard's Court cottages, occupied (and fondly remembered by some) until fairly recently. The medieval trefoil headed window in one wall is, however, a recent addition, having been moved here from 75 High Street when that building was demolished in 1983.

52 High Street

This is a grade II listed building, the present frontage having been built in the early 19th century.

In the 18th century this, together with No 54, was assessed for tax as a dwelling house and coach house. As part of the Pierce Cornish estate it was known as the *White Hart Inn* (1759: innkeeper, Emanuel Parcel) and then became the house of Cornish's sister Ann, 'a lunatic', and her attendants, before being sold off on the bankruptcy of Cornish's heir John Wilson in 1768.

During the 19th century, No 52 was owned by Edward Ballard - a prominent citizen, ironmonger, landowner and alderman. The adjoining court with its cottages (some of which still exist today at the rear of the building) was known as Ballard's Court, though for some time it was also called Walters Court after one of its residents - Henry Walters 'the Cowbridge hermit'. He was the son of the Revd John Walters of Llandough who had compiled the first Anglo-Welsh dictionary, and the brother of two headmasters of the Grammar School; Henry's unkempt appearance belied his erudition. He tried to establish a printing business here in the 1780s.

No 52 was let to Thomas Miles as a grocer's shop around 1851, and to John Howe, butcher and grocer, and then his widow Mary for the remainder of the 19th century. George Mitchell took over the shop in the 1900s. More recent occupants have been Nanette's wool shop and now Quills stationers and art materials, with Marooned haircutters above.

50 and 50a High Street

This is a grade II listed building and records of the 17th century suggest that this plot housed an inn, with 'brewhouse, furnaces, vats and cooling vats', before being cited as 'the mansion house on the market place' in 1700. It was owned by the Aubreys, landed gentry, but transferred to the Cornish family on the breakdown of the marriage of Cecil Aubrey and Edward Portrey. By the mid 18th century, it was known as the *Half Moon*. Thomas Emanuel was the landlord, and there were two barbers' shops within. Its owner went bankrupt by 1768, and for a while the house was used only as a private residence.

In the 19th century, it housed the draper's shop first of David Prichard, then of Samuel David Evans who established his clothing 'emporium' here by 1861 before moving it across the street to Nos 37/39. Miss Ann Davis was here in 1871 with the stationery shop that she had started with her brother Ebenezer in No 43, later transferring it to 70 Eastgate.There was another draper's, then a butcher's, before W E Jones made it his cycle depot around 1912. Walter Knapton, Cowbridge photographer, occupied the upper floor: many of the old postcards of Cowbridge seem to have been taken from the first floor windows.

During the 1950s and 60s, this was the Grammar School's tuck shop and cafe (Westcotts), the boys not being allowed further into the town for refreshments. A dentist was upstairs. The building later became a pharmacy and then a delicatessen, before becoming the present En Vogue and Goose Island dress shops.

Church Street

This street contains two grade II listed cottages, once a two-unit house dating from the mid-16th century and still having an original stone arched doorway.

It is a short but important street, which led from the former Guild Hall and market place, not only to the church and grammar school, but also through the South Gate, past the tollgate cottage and down to the town mill. It was formerly much busier than it is today. Nine houses lined the west side, five having been demolished when the *Duke of Wellington* car park was created in the 1940s, and two others - one substantial - which were bought by the school in 1868 were knocked down to create a play area 30 years later. At that time, the borough pound (for stray animals) lay within the gate on the west.

The property on the western corner, by High Street, was a leather work-er's for almost two centuries. Daniel Morgan, cobbler, was here in 1767, his house adjoining the *Half Moon Inn* on High Street. In 1843, Nathaniel Llewellyn was running his saddlery business, which was continued after his premature death until the 1880s by his widow Jane, assisted by some of their many children. 'Thomas the saddler' was here in 1908, and later cobbler Solomon Andrews, known as 'Nobby' the tin-tack swallower, and said to be as tiny as Rumpelstiltskin.

There were other saddlers and shoemakers, as well as butchers, curriers, gardeners, and a 'rural postman' among the residents of the street during the 19th century. Hannah Howe who lived in 1861 in one of the cottages still existing today, was Cowbridge's last hand-loom weaver. In 1871, David Davis, bookbinder, occupied one of the two corporation houses, and in 1891, John Evans, tailor, lived and had his workshop in one of the two larger houses at the High Street end. He was choirmaster at Ramoth Baptist chapel.

In 1662, an almshouse had stood on the east side, close to the present day *Duke of Wellington* ballroom. A slaughterhouse was later built in this area. By the 19th century, a small row of cottages ('Johnny the Backers') stood at right angles to the street, served by a lane where the entrance to the Country Pine Warehouse is today.

The Grammar School

A Cowbridge tailor named Toolye owned this site between church, town walls and Church Street at the turn of the 17th century: it was bought by Sir Edward and Sir John Stradling of St Donats, who established the Free School here. The school and many of the Stradling lands in the Vale of Glamorgan were acquired by Sir Leoline Jenkins - an illustrious 'Old Boy' who had become Secretary of State to Charles II - and then bequeathed by him to Jesus College, Oxford, thereby ensuring the financial security of Jesus College and beginning the long connection between the school and the college.

Until 1847 the school was a modest building, with initially one school room for all ages of pupils; its mode of construction would have been similar to that of the 'boothouse', now standing dilapidated in the school yard east of the South Gate.

A rebuilding in Gothic style took place in 1848 - Prichard the architect attempting to create some harmony between the school and the ancient houses in Church Street, the South Gate, and the church. The neatly cut lawn surrounded by flowerbeds and enclosed by the building and two raised banks created an impression of an Oxbridge college; and indeed the school was particularly successful in preparing students for Oxbridge and other universities. Two old boys (who went to neither) were Alun Lewis, highly regarded as a war poet, and Anthony Hopkins the actor.

As a boarding school, there were three dormitories which could not have changed a great deal since 1848; boarding ceased soon after the school went comprehensive in 1974, and the school building fell out of use soon after.

The Church of the Holy Cross

The church was built soon after the 'new town' of Cowbridge was created, and much of the nave, tower and chancel dates from the late 13th century. The shape of the tower suggests that it was intended to serve as a stronghold or watchtower; Iolo Morganwg stated that it was once topped with a spire.

The slim pillars separating the nave from the south aisle were put up when the south or Llanquian aisle was constructed, reputedly as a gift in 1473 from Lady Anne Neville, wife of Richard III. The concrete bases to the pillars date from a 1926 reconstruction. Another link with Richard III was his granting of a chaplaincy to Holy Cross church in 1484; a copy of that charter is displayed in the church.

Memorials in the church (for many were buried here) date back to the 17th century: the most spectacular wall monument is that to the Carne family in the south aisle. Others commemorated include Judge David Jenkins (a Royalist who was imprisoned in the Tower of London in the Civil War), a multiplicity of headmasters of the Grammar School, and the Edmondes family of Old Hall.

The close links between school and church (daily attendance at church was compulsory for pupils in the early 20th century, and headmasters prior to 1918 were all clerics) are also shown by the stained glass windows of benefactors, and the school war memorial window.

There is a fine peal of eight bells, cast in 1722 in the Evans foundry of Chepstow, which are rung regularly.

48 High Street – Duke of Wellington

This grade II listed building still retains its original entrance passageway which separates the public bar from the small room on the left, and upstairs, a fine fireplace. The front part is of 17th century origin, but the lounge bar and ballroom are late 19th century additions. The ballroom floor is supported by beams made from the masts of a ship, the Ben Gloe, which was wrecked off Marcross in 1884.

In 1662, this burgage plot contained 'a messuage, stable, brewhouse and garden' belonging to Rice Portrey of Boverton, leased to Margaret Seys of Cowbridge. Ninety years later there is a mention of the property being the house of Pierce Cornish (not necessarily an inn at this time, as many larger houses had their own brewhouses), ownership passing by 1784 to Walter Williams with William Overs as tenant. There was then a variety of owners and tenants, and it became known as the *Black Horse* in 1827. There is uncertainty over the reason for the change of name later to the *Duke of Wellington*. It was still the *Black Horse* in 1830, many years after Waterloo, so it was probably named after Wellington's death in 1852.

By 1848, the inn was owned by Edward Ballard, whose warehouse was where the lounge is now situated. Of the 19th century tenants, David and Ann Thomas were innkeepers for about 20 years, and were followed by the Spencers – Thomas, Margaret and Arthur, who were here from at least 1891 to 1919.

Ownership passed to S A Brain and Co in 1919; the first licensee under the new owners was Thomas Pratt who is still remembered affectionately.

46 High Street

Photographs of this part of the High Street taken about 1900 show three adjoining buildings all looking very much as the *Duke of Wellington* does today. This, the middle one, was the *Cowbridge Arms* at that time, though we can trace the history back much earlier.

Owned in 1662 by Sir Edward Thomas of Llanmihangel, it remained in the ownership of the Thomas/Wyndham family until the early 20th century. It was leased to David Bowen of Swansea, a clockmaker specialising in long case clocks, in 1751 as 'one bakehouse, one garden, two curtilages and one penthouse, formerly in the occupation of Catherine Richard and now of Mary Llewellin, widow'. The bakehouse became a beerhouse, known first as the *Half Moon* around 1815 when Jenkin Morris, maltster of St Hilary, was the tenant (the same name had been used at 50 High Street earlier) - and then the *Cowbridge Arms* by 1827.

The innkeeper from 1827 to 1851 was Thomas Griffiths, then Mary Reynolds in 1861 and Morgan Thomas, innkeeper and butcher, in 1871 - followed by his widow in 1881 and 1891, with his son Watkin Thomas as assistant brewer in the latter year. With the death of Margaret Thomas in 1902 the frequency of change in leaseholder and occupier accelerated. The *Cowbridge Arms* was purchased from the Wyndhams by Sarah Labdon in 1919, but by the time of its sale to Arthur Mills in 1928 it was described as 'formerly used as an inn but now unlicensed'. Part was then used as an extension to the Cowbridge Garage Co next door, and part for the South Wales Power Co (later SWEB). Current users are Ushi, a gift shop, and the Tenovus charity shop.

44 High Street

Throughout the 18th century and into the 19th this property was owned by the Carne family. A 1704 document refers to its lease 'to Margaret Williams, lately in the occupation of William Freame of Cowbridge' and a lease in 1768 to John Edmondes records 'lately leased by Catherine Williams, now in occupation of Mary Llewellin and Richard Hodgson'.

By 1787 this had become yet another of Cowbridge's inns, the *White Lion*, which was described in John Carne's accounts as 'a house set in the market place opposite the east end of the Town Hall', and was let to Joseph Kayes, a currier and leather cutter. He became the first of four such craftsmen, who prepared leather for saddlery and shoe-making, on the site until 1901. (The building's role as an inn ceased early in the 19th century.) The other curriers were John Kayes, John Davies, and Edward Davies, who was here from 1848 to the end of the century, though it seems that the currier business had finished before 1891.

The redevelopment of the site, from a low two-storey building to the dominant half-timbered structure we see today, was the work of A T Mills, from Cardiff, who set up the Cowbridge Garage Company here, and sold bicycles and cars. Subsequently the motor business was carried on by Vospers and then by A E Harris, the main Ford dealer, into the 1960s. Frequent ownership changes (the Co-op Jumbo store did not last long) followed with the development of small retail outlets. Today the building is occupied by Italus shoes and Valentino's restaurant, with the Conservative club above.

40 and 42 High Street

This is a grade II listed building of 17th century, or earlier, origin. It is very likely that this was the *Angel Inn* occupied by William Freame, a Cowbridge alderman, at the end of the 17th century. It was certainly owned by Francis Gwyn at that time, and remained in the hands of the Gwyn family (of Llansannor) until 1800, at which time Morgan David was the tenant.

By 1808, Isaiah Verity was the owner. It was then the *White Hart Inn*, still with Morgan David as the innkeeper, and he remained as landlord until 1825. Thomas Griffiths, the last known landlord of the *White Hart*, bought the property from the Veritys, but then had a number of tenants (John Parsons in 1843, Frederick Smyth, an ironmonger from Carmarthen, in 1851) before moving in himself. He died here in 1862, leaving his estate in trust for his wife and three children.

In 1881, Richard Pickard ran a grocer's shop here, having moved with his wife and three children from No 79. His sons, John, then a cabinet maker, and William, eventually went on to run their own shop in Eastgate, so by 1891 Richard lived in this house with just his wife and daughter.

No 40 was occupied by E C Gibbs, stationer, in 1912; Charles Symes, a confectioner, occupied No 42. After the second world war, the building housed Campbell's tea room, a tiny cafe. Mrs Campbell married Glyn Roberts who opened a delicatessen here, which later became L'Epicure. Today it houses Thresher, wine merchants, and Etcetera, fine leather goods.

36 and 38 High Street

This is a grade II listed building, with a fine example of a medieval warehouse at the rear of No 38 - the internal pigeon nesting holes make a most interesting feature of the residential accommodation here today. This was originally a Carne property of considerable size and importance, paying 9/- land tax in 1773. The date of 1832 inscribed over the arch points to a rebuilding - or perhaps just the building of an 'extension' over the arch.

Throughout the 19th century, the building was divided into two properties. The western half, at least from 1843, contained a chemist's shop, run until after 1871 by the most appropriately named Thomas Lister. He was from Carmarthen; his nephew, John Llewellyn, after serving his apprenticeship in the shop, ran it after him from the 1870s - and still lived here in 1921. The other part of the building had a variety of tenants - John Lee in 1843; John King, a 'funded proprietor and railway shareholder' from Middlesex with wife and three daughters in 1851 and 1861; Thomas Matthews, a retired saddler, moved in from 65 High Street and was here in 1881 and 1891.

In 1922, this was one of the properties conveyed for the benefit of the Grammar School by Sir Thomas Mansel Franklen of St Hilary (the Franklens had taken over the property from the Carnes in the late 18th century). The TM Franklen trust still exists to give financial help to pupils of Cowbridge School, but it does not seem to have gained a great deal from the sale of this building in 1942.

Today, the ground floor shops are occupied by Woodcocks boutique and Davies's newsagents, with residential accommodation above.

32 and 34 High Street - Great House

This grade II listed building is of 16th to 17th century origin, but the frontage with its Venetian windows was altered in the 18th century. Earlier windows are visible at the rear of the property, through the coach-entrance, and also on the stairs of the adjoining 30 High Street, which was built much later.

Great House was the town house of the Carne family of Nash Manor. A deed of 1620 relates to Carne's mansion house in Cowbridge, and Thomas Carne was recorded as paying hearth tax on seven hearths in 1670. In 1763 the house (and 'garden, orchard, stable, brewhouse and curtilages') was sold by the Revd John Carne to the Revd Daniel Durel, headmaster of Cowbridge Grammar School; his daughter married John Franklen of Clemenstone, and the house remained in the ownership of the Franklen family until the 20th century.

In the 19th century Great House was occupied by a succession of private householders, although from about 1860 it was divided into two properties. Chemists - John Thomas and W J Evans among them - occupied the western half, while the eastern part held a girls' school, run first by Ellen Thorne and Miss Hill, and then, from the 1880s, by Anne Culverwell and her daughters. Some floral panels painted by the pupils can be seen in the pharmacy today.

In 1922, Sir Thomas Franklen gave Great House (and the tennis court below the churchyard) to Cowbridge School, and Franklen House (No 32) opened as a boarding house of the Grammar School in 1926. It was, however, closed as a boarding house in 1939, and the whole property sold in 1942. Today it contains two residential properties as well as Great House Pharmacy.

16 to 30 High Street

These are all grade II listed buildings, included for their group value, rather than for specific architectural features.

The seven properties numbered 16 to 30 form a terrace of houses built on land originally belonging to the Carnes and which had been part of the Great House garden. This was sold or leased by Richard Franklen of Great House in the 1830s and 1840s. The five two-storey houses are bounded at each end by a three-storey house (No 16 and No 30).

The conditions of the leases imposed by Franklen were fairly stringent: the main woods to be used were to be of oak or Memel deal (Baltic pine), and the buildings were to be roofed with Caernarfon slates. It appears from the deeds that the original intention was to have houses of uniform height throughout - the protruding stones at third floor level on Nos 16 and 30 also suggest this.

A right of way, ten feet wide, was to allow access to the rear of the premises for horses, carriages and people - this is via the arch between Nos 22 and 26.

Details of the individual properties are found on succeeding pages.

30 and 28 High Street

30 High Street: This early 19th century three-storey building was erected by Robert Stibbs, confectioner, on land leased from Richard Franklen of Great House. It must have been with Franklen's permission that this building blocked off the east-facing ground floor window of Great House, now visible when ascending to R C Morgan, dental surgeon, on the first floor.

The property has shown remarkable continuity of use: the Stibbs family ran a bakery here throughout the 19th century; C M Davies ('Charlie the Bun'), who became mayor of the town, took over in the early 1900s. Mrs Webb ran a grocery store here in the 1960s. Now the Ogmore Vale Bakery has revived the earlier bakery specialisation.

28 High Street: For most of the 19th century this property was occupied by boot and shoe-makers who employed between three and six men. In 1851, 23-year-old Thomas Williams was the boot maker, but by 1861 he had been replaced by his father, also Thomas Williams, and in 1871 both were in residence.

In 1881, David Giles, previously a bootmaker living in West Village, was head of household but by 1891 the premises were used by John Morgan, butcher. In 1912 they were occupied by William Henry John, in the 1960s Harrison Electrical, and today are the Principality Building Society office.

26 and 24 High Street

26 High Street. From its construction in 1842, this was a blacksmith's shop, owned and occupied by successive generations of the Griffiths family. The forge was at the rear of the High Street, accessed through the archway. In 1844 the smith was John Griffiths who had inherited the business (then in the Limes) from his father Thomas Griffiths on his death in 1831. In 1851 John Griffiths was a widower with two daughters but he remarried before 1854 and then fathered a family of three more daughters, and three sons all of whom became blacksmiths. The eldest son, John Griffiths jnr, had taken over the business by 1881 when he was assisted by his two brothers, Thomas and William. John Griffiths died at the age of 40 in 1896 and in 1912 the premises were occupied by Durston the butcher. A newsagents (Simkins, then Hollings) in the 1960s and 70s, it is now again a butcher's shop - Nicholas's.

24 High Street. Despite the address, this is not in the High Street at all! About 1884 Robert Newman from Moreton-in-Marsh, Gloucestershire with his wife Caroline, moved to Cowbridge where their first five children were born. By 1891 the family were living in this cottage reached via the arch between Nos 22 and 26. It had been built to the south of the rear boundary of the *Royal Oak* and on the edge of the triangular garden plot. Robert's occupation is given as market gardener in the 1891 census, and he certainly cultivated that garden until it became part of the Birds' garden centre. His donkey (used to carry the vegetables for sale) was a well-loved animal in Cowbridge in the early years of the century. The house is still occupied by members of the Newman family.

22 High Street

This property was built by Thomas Lewis, a market gardener in 1841, when a 99-year lease from Richard Franklen to Lewis was signed. Thomas Lewis, born in Penllyn, had moved around before settling in Cowbridge where his youngest child, Marianne, was born in 1840. His son David was born in Colwinston in 1832 and twins, Catherine and Margaret were born in Newton Nottage in 1835.

In the 1851 to 1871 census returns, Thomas Lewis's occupation was given as 'market gardener of half an acre of ground' - probably the triangular piece of land to the rear of the High Street, on which Birds' lawnmower workshop is now sited. Thomas Lewis's wife, Anne, was a dealer in china and earthenware at which her daughter, Mary Anne (or Annie) assisted her. By 1874 Annie Lewis had inherited the business and before 1881 she was married to Thomas Davies of Pencoed. He continued with the market garden until 1889 when No 22 was sold to John Jones ('gardener and earthenware dealer') while Thomas Davies moved to Penprisk, Pencoed.

In 1912 both china shop and market gardener had gone and Arthur Sanders, bootmaker (who subsequently moved over the road) lived here. In 1939/40, the shop became the Milk Bar, with Mrs Gwendoline Tilley as proprietress. Today it houses Kim's Chinese Kitchen, a Chinese take-away.

20 and 18 High Street

20 High Street was a licensed premises called the *Royal Oak* throughout the 19th century. In 1844 and 1851 the licensee was Morgan Williams who bought the land from Richard Franklen and built the property. Like most landlords at this time, he also had a trade, that of wheelwright and carpenter.

Morgan Williams was replaced by David Williams (apparently not related) in 1861. David Williams was also an omnibus driver: horse-drawn omnibuses linked with Cardiff, Pontypridd and the South Wales Railway. By 1891 the licence was held by David Williams's widow, Mary, their only son William still living at home and working as a draper's assistant. In 1912 the licensee was William Thomas, Thomas the Carrier, who also delivered goods from Cowbridge station. It is today the office of Gaskell and Walker, solicitors.

18 High Street was built in two parts - the eastern part by Richard Rees, a mason, and sub-let to Thomas Davies, a surgeon, in 1836, while the western plot was leased directly to Davies who built the rest of the building two years later. Davies had died by 1844 and the house - still owned by Richard Franklen - was occupied by his widow, Mary Davies; it was empty in 1851.

A watchmaker, Henry Johnson, was living here in 1861, 1871 and 1881, with his sister and his daughter Sarah. In 1891 Richard Watkins, a tailor, with family and apprentices, made up a household of nine residents, and continued trading at least until 1928. Ken George had his tailor's shop here in the 1960s and 70s. Today it houses Jon Ian shoes, Tapes video shop and The Hair Business above.

16 High Street

Built in 1833 by Richard Rees, a Cowbridge mason, the house changed hands fairly rapidly. In 1844 it was occupied by William John, but by 1851 it was a beerhouse known as the *Farmers Arms*, the licensee William Hopkin from Ystradowen. By 1861 the licence had gone and the property was occupied by Samuel Warren, cabinet maker and painter, originally from Dorset. His young wife Hannah died after the birth of their fourth child, who also died. Samuel remarried, his second wife being Elizabeth, the daughter of John Griffiths the blacksmith at No 26, and had two more children, but in 1865 Samuel died and his widow moved back to her parents' home. It has recently come to light that their surviving son, also Samuel, must have emigrated to the USA, there marrying one of the daughters of emigrant Ebenezer Davis (of 43 High Street).

A later resident, William Williams, also a cabinet maker with a wife and four young children, died aged 40 in 1874, and his wife died the following year. Their youngest child, six-year-old Honor Alice Williams, was adopted by their next-door neighbours Nathaniel and Anna Bird.

In 1881 a widow, Annie Lewis, with the help of her two eldest daughters and her dressmaking skills, was supporting six children, aged from two to 15. The house was comparatively empty in 1891, with just a dress-maker, a tailor and a young apprentice. By 1912, William Davies had his newsagents and stationers shop here, while in the 1960s and 70s it was Oakleys the butchers. It now houses Pabi, a dress shop, and the High Street Jewellers.

14 High Street

A deed in the Glamorgan Record Office identifies this site in 1787 as an inn or alehouse called *The Lamb* adjoining the town wall, but throughout the 19th century this was an ironmongery business in the ownership of the Bird family.

The business was founded in 1796 when 23-year-old Edward Bird of Cardiff purchased the property and the meadow known as Waun-y-gaer. By 1841 his younger brother James was the owner. In 1812 James had married a local girl, Sarah Young, daughter of Nathaniel Young the licensee of the *Greyhound Inn*. Sarah died in 1837 but James continued living over the shop for a further 20 years. While his father was alive, his youngest son, Nathaniel, was the Cowbridge postmaster, but when James Bird died, at the age of 81 in 1857, Nathaniel succeeded him in the business. Nathaniel was a prominent member of the borough council and donated £500 towards the cost of erecting the Cowbridge Institute at the rear of the Town Hall (which was opened in 1895 more than two years after Nathaniel's death). Nathaniel and his wife Anna were childless and the business was inherited by James G Harold Bird, son of Nathaniel's elder brother James.

In the late 1970s the three-storey building fronting on to the High Street was demolished and rebuilt with a similar facade to the original building. It is now occupied by Martin the newsagent with Hurran's Garden Centre and Birds' mower repair workshops to the rear. The plaque on the front of the building suggests that Iolo Morganwg had a shop here (and there is a sample of the script he invented).

10 High Street

This inn, until recently the *Master Brewer*, has also been known as the *Butchers Arms* and the *Red Dragon*.

In 1843, this was one of Edward Ballard's many properties in the town; the publican was David Morgan, who is shown in the 1851 census as being in addition a butcher - one of those selling their meat from the stalls in the shambles, next to the Town Hall, as there were no butchers' shops in the town at that time. Morgan came from Llanblethian Farm, and had married Ann Thomas in 1835; they had four children by 1840. By 1851, however, Ann had died and David had a second wife, Gwenllian - they lived in the *Butchers Arms* until David's death in 1873, and Gwenllian continued running the public house to the 1880s. The owner by then was Lord Dynevor.

After this long period of stability in tenancy, there were some rapid changes. Thomas Loughor appears as publican in 1891, but by 1894 the licensee was Lewis Jenkins, of the Cowbridge Brewery, and then his widow Ann from 1897. Once ownership had passed (via John George, a coal merchant) to Hansard Brothers in 1900, and then to Thomas Morgan of the Pontyclun Brewery, there was a rapid succession of occupants, but Samuel Hayter was here for over eight years, to 1912, before moving across to the *Horse and Groom*.

One celebrated landlord in the mid 20th century, by which time the name had changed to the *Red Dragon*, was Jimmy Blair, the ex-Cardiff City goalkeeper.

4 to 8 High Street

The building now housing Eastgate Antiques and the adjoining shop was in the 19th century an inn, the *Ship Aground*. The tithe map of 1843 gives the owner and occupier as Mary Jones, who was followed in 1851 by Teresa Jones, possibly her daughter. When Owen Roberts was the landlord in 1861, there were ten residents, aged from 79 to one year old. From 1865 to 1871 the name appears to have changed to the *Cross Keys*, occupied by Thomas David with his wife Margaret and daughter Jane plus their lodger Thomas Briton, a widowed tailor from Oxford. The census of 1881 reveals a change of use to a seed and wool stores in the possession of Frederick Miles and his family who were still in occupation in 1891. Mrs Miles was a grocer here in 1912.

Post war the building housed Westons grocery shop and then Woods greengrocers, while the next-door property was Victor Grubb's barber's shop before it became Bettina, a dress shop.

Even the car-park to the east formerly contained a building of interest. It was a Wesleyan chapel from 1780 to 1895 (when a new chapel was opened in Eastgate), became an armoury in the Boer War, and then a Navvies' Mission. On the forecourt, boys used to play cricket. (Ralph Bird said that if a ball was hit into the ivy on the *Blue Bell* wall, Mr Miles the grocer would come to adjudicate whether or not the batsman was out!) Later it was used for Mr A S Evans' garage and eventually a post office garage. The building was demolished when the supermarket was built.

2 High Street - Filco

It is sad to think that until fairly recently a listed building with a Tudor arched doorway, the *Blue Bell Inn*, stood on this site. The building itself – admittedly in poor condition – was demolished to allow the construction of a supermarket which is hardly an architectural masterpiece.

The earliest reference to the *Blue Bell* found in the Edmondes family papers is dated 1745 when Mary Williams covenanted 'to buy all malt from Thomas Edmondes so long as she keeps the *Blue Bell* as a public house'. In addition, this document shows that the *Blue Bell* was associated with a tan house (or tannery), and that the property had been bought by Thomas Edmondes from William Davies, a scholar of Jesus College, Oxford (who had been left the property by his grandfather, another William Davies). John Edmondes, the next owner, pursued the debts owed to him with zeal, as in the case of Ann Evan of the *Blue Bell* in 1766. She owed three years rent of £15, and so her goods and chattels were sold to pay her debts.

There were relatively few changes in occupancy – Francis Thomas was the tenant from 1777 to past 1800, and then a Jennet Thomas from 1827 to 1851. Richard Howe, a butcher, had taken over by 1858, and his wife Elizabeth was still running the inn in 1871. William Williams and his wife were then in charge for another 20 years and, after the brief tenancy of Mary Ann Harries, Michael Fitzgerald ran the inn from 1906 to 1920. Other than these changes in tenancy the *Blue Bell* remained virtually unaltered until well into the 20th century. Tales are still told of the regulars sitting in the bar, as late as the 1920s, with their feet immersed in flood waters from the River Thaw.

The Limes

The first reference to lime kilns here was in 1760, on land owned by the Wyndhams, but in 1614 the Dynevor estate owned 'the lymes and two orchards' where stood a 'mansion house' occupied by Reece Knapp. This was probably where the two houses are today, facing the visitor entering the Limes road. Further records relate to a large house here, leased by the Carnes to Ann Cadogan in 1753, which she had passed on to her niece Mary Morgan by 1784. In the same period, Thomas Edmondes was leasing to Edward Ballard, skinner, his 'courtyard and wainhouse', in the area where the garage now stands.

In 1817, Thomas Griffiths, blacksmith, who later moved to 26 High Street, had his shop on the eastern side, towards Eastgate, and in 1822 Robert Hillier, linen draper, built the adjoining cottage. The following year, the Revd Edward Morgan of Verlands House leased land to David John for a house and garden on the far western side, backing on to the river, with 'a plantation of fir trees' alongside.

In 1825, the Sion Calvinistic Methodist chapel was built (now converted into flats), around the corner of the Limes road. Later the Cory family converted a stable into a hall for English Methodist services, eventually used by the Sons of Temperance Society. This is now Joseph's Coat patchwork shop. Thomas Nicholas, timber merchant, operated his thriving business in the eastern Limes, and the Cowbridge Gas Light and Coke Company built the gasworks in 1851 behind the former 'mansion house' - so that the town was lit by 20 street lamps by 1855.

A row of cottages by now lined the river at the bridge - one was used later for a laundry business - with a continuous row on the eastern side. By 1891 there were 21 cottages in the Limes, inhabited mainly by labourers and railway workers with some families from Ireland. Around the turn of the century, the Tuckers had a china and earthenware shop at the entrance where the garage now stands, this being later used as a waste-paper store.

The first Bridge Garage was built about 1915 by Mr Arthur Evans. Just after the second world war, when cars were reappearing in the show-rooms, there was a disastrous fire here, destroying the garage and the long-awaited cars. The river was diverted about 1950 to its present course; the gas works was demolished in the 1950s and the present Limes Court flats built on the site.

72 and 74 Eastgate

For much of the 18th century No 72 was owned by the wealthy Bates family and leased to a variety of tenants - William Preece in the 1770s and 80s, Humphrey Salter a hairdresser in the 1790s, and John Aubrey a cabinet maker in 1800. In 1822 the lease was assigned to William Williams, a tiler and plasterer. Even though Edward Bates, a surgeon, died in 1849, the connection with the family continued as his widow, daughter and grand-daughter - perhaps then in more straightened circumstances - lived in the house in 1861.

A major change of use occurred from the late 1860s until the mid 1920s, when the building became known as the *Bridge Inn* - it stood close to the old bridge over the river. (A chain-pump to pump water from the river stood on the bridge parapet until a new bridge was constructed in 1911). The public house was kept for over 40 years by master house-painter Solomon Warren, originally from Dorset. He brought up five children here, his eldest son John running the town's brass band and using the large upstairs room for practices. The Crowleys, from Ireland, took over the inn early in the 20th century and held lively 'hooleys' in its parlour.

The *Glamorgan Gazette* of 11th June 1920 reported that Sergeant Thomas found Sidney Taylor sitting down in the *Bridge Inn* on a Sunday with half a pint of beer before him. The Crowleys were fined £2 for permitting consumption of intoxicating liquor on Sunday. The inn closed and from 1923 it became a plumber's workshop. Since the 1980s it has housed the Cowbridge Bookshop, Oops a Daisy florists and Makers craft co-operative (earlier a pottery).

70 Eastgate

Reputedly the location of Rhys Thomas' printing works in 1770, by the late 18th century this grade II listed building was a private house owned by Elizabeth Williams with a number of different tenants. By 1815 Robert Hillier owned and lived in the house, and by 1830 Mary Howell had taken over, and was still here in 1843.

It was a grocer's shop in the mid 19th century (the tenant in 1851 and 1861 being Isabella Roberts, born in Brampton, Northants, with a son who had been born in Ireland and another son and a daughter born in Llantwit Major - a mobile family indeed!). She was succeeded by 1871 by Catherine Thomas, another grocer, but this time born in Cowbridge. Miss Ann Davis lived here from the 1880s, running a stationer's and newsagent's shop after starting this trade with her brother Ebenezer at 43 High Street. She went on to publish the fascinating book 'Sixty One Views of Cowbridge and District' in which she and her shop are portrayed.

In the early 20th century, Albert Maddox and his wife ran a fried fish shop here, but rather more importantly he also operated an early bus service for the town. He started first with a horse-drawn wagonette, driving parties to the races and to the seaside, but from 1914 provided a weekly service to Cardiff and changed to motor transport. The enterprise faded away in the 1920s.

Over the latter part of the 20th century, No 70 was mainly a gift and kitchenware shop - Bridge Studio - with residential accommodation above. Square Spots, a dress shop, occupies the eastern part.

60 Eastgate

Ball tennis courts, where the game was played with bare hands and a hard ball, existed in most Glamorgan towns during the 18th century. This was the site of the Cowbridge court, its high stone wall backing on to the road, and an inn (the *Three Tuns*) adjoining on the west. Thomas Edmondes rebuilt the property about 1750 and had his malthouse at the rear, backing on to the 'Stumpy fields'.

From about 1858 to 1921, the inn, known also as the *Tennis Court*, was kept by the Aubrey family. The first Richard Aubrey, a wheelwright of some renown, was said to have invented a three-wheeled velocipede in the early 1900s: this came to a sticky end at its trial on Stalling Down above the town. The second Richard Aubrey was also a wheelwright, so it is not surprising that the inn became the *Wheelwrights Arms* until it was sold in 1922 to A T Mills, the garage proprietor of 44 High St.

He transformed the whole plot into the Pavilion Cinema. In 1925, it opened in grand style with a maple-floored ballroom upstairs and the cinema below. Many society functions were held here: in 1933, for example, Lloyd George was dined and presented with the freedom of the borough. In 1942 the building was almost entirely destroyed by fire. The local cinema owner, Philip Phillips, rebuilt it as a cinema seating 200, and it operated as such until the 1950s when it lost its former glory and became the council's depot for refuse lorries. In the 1990s, after local protest that the facade be preserved as a town landmark, it was redesigned for office use.

54 Eastgate - Heath House

The first recorded occupants of the house, a grade II listed building, were Edward and Mary Morgan in 1717. Edward Morgan was a 'cordwainer' as shoemakers were described at that time. At that date, the house was mortgaged to a widow called Joan John or Jones and having acquired the house she was living here in 1722. She died in 1724 and left the house to her daughter Mary and son-in-law Edmund Kemeys, who was born in 1663.

The Kemeys family was large, with several members established in both Cowbridge and Llanblethian. A John Kemeys is recorded as holding a lot of land in both places in 1570. It was also a Kemeys who married Evan Jenkins, the brother of Sir Leoline Jenkins, the 17th century statesman and benefactor of Cowbridge Grammar School.

Some time after 1738 the house was acquired by Nathaniel Taynton who died in 1754. He left the house to his widow Joan Taynton who in 1765 leased it to another widow named Jennet Llewellyn. Her daughter Catherine had married Henry Lloyd of Coity, and when Jennet Llewellyn died in 1773 she left the house to Catherine and her elder sister Frances. The Lloyds came to live here between 1784 and 1789.

The owner and occupier at the end of the 18th century was Morgan Williams who was listed in the Universal British Directory of 1793 as one of the 12 gentry of Cowbridge. He was also a freeman of the town.

By 1816 the house was owned by a solicitor, Thomas Llewellyn Williams. He had died by 1818, when he left the house to his son who had exactly the same name and was also a solicitor. Both were freemen of Cowbridge. The son married Frances Williams, born in Margam in 1801, and they rented the house to a succession of tenants. After her husband died in

1844, Frances returned to live in the house with her widowed sister, Catherine Thomas.

Christina Ord had previously lived in Llanblethian and had suffered a series of tragedies when five of her seven children died before they were 30, and her husband, Ralph, died in Australia in 1860. In 1869 she moved here with her two remaining sons. Edward, the eldest, later became well established as a Cowbridge solicitor in Caercady House.

In 1872, Owen and Catherine Davies, with their five children, came to live here. Owen Davies worked at the National and Provincial Bank (now the National Westminster) but he was also a poet, writing under the name of 'Eos Afan' (the Nightingale of Afan). In April 1873 he was chairman of the Cowbridge Eisteddfod, for which a temporary wooden building which accommodated 8000 people was erected in the Bear Field.

In the 1890s, Heath House became a small boarding school run by the Llewellyn sisters, and founded by Annie Llewellyn, the daughter of Nathaniel Llewellyn the saddler of Church Street, who had died in 1855 leaving his widow to bring up a large family. Annie, born in 1849, had been one of the 'First Orphans' selected for an education at the new Howell's School in Llandaff, which opened in 1860. Her ambition was to run her own school, and by 1871 she had set one up in her mother's home in Church Street, later moving it to 5 High Street, and then to Heath House. Annie closed her school here in the early 1900s - soon after the Girls' High School had opened.

In 1910 the house was purchased by Annie Giles, who, with her husband William had previously lived in the Limes. He was a commission agent and haulage contractor, and his horses and carts were stabled at what is now Quarry House on the Cardiff road. The house is today a private residence.

48 Eastgate - East Villa

This grade II listed building has an 18th to early 19th century facade to a probably earlier core. There is a typical joint-lined stucco front with a very wide external chimney breast to the north-west gable wall. This represents the remains of a stable demolished in the 1880s (described in 1773 as 'Mr Collins wash house, now a stable'). There is a semi-circular front doorway with moulded architrave, open pediment with modillions on pilasters, panelled reveals, and fanlight with tracery. The interior contains contemporary ground floor window shutters and a staircase with slender circular newel at its foot.

In 1784 the house was occupied by Jane Vallance (whose daughter was probably the Jane Vallance described as 'the beauty of Wales' in the diary of William Thomas) and in the 1790s by Miss Savours. William James lived here in the 1830s and 40s. In 1851 James Taylor, a landed proprietor and fund holder (connected with Cowbridge Mill), was in occupation and from the 1860s to the mid 1880s Charlotte and Louisa Edmondes lived here. They were the unmarried daughters of Major Thomas Edmondes and sisters of the Revd Thomas Edmondes of Old Hall. There are commemorative panels to both sisters at Holy Cross church. The Edmondes family ended their association with the property with its sale by the Venerable Frederick Edmondes of Nolton Court, Bridgend, in 1914, to two sisters, Bertha and Margaret Williams.

After a period of commercial ownership from 1973 to 1993 (Louis C Fisher Ltd), the house has now reverted to a private residence.

46 Eastgate - The Armoury

This grade II listed building has an early 19th century frontage of four bays with joint-lined stucco. There is a square-headed doorway in the third bay from the left with a moulded flat cornice hood on half-round columns.

In 1784 the house seems to have been linked with No 48 as it also was occupied by Jane Vallance. By the 1790s, however, they were separate, with John Thomas, a cooper, living here. In 1851 a coach builder, Morgan Edwards, lived here and he was followed in 1861 by Evan Jones, a painter, plumber and Wesleyan local preacher (with his wife and four children).

A tombstone in Holy Cross church is 'in memory of John Williams, Esq, of the Armoury, who died 5 Dec 1867 in his 65th year'. He was the son of the Revd William Williams, DD, headmaster of Cowbridge Grammar School and brother-in-law of the Revd Thomas Edmondes of Old Hall. By 1870 the house was occupied by his brother William Williams, a wine merchant, who had moved from The Poplars near the church. William Williams died in 1885 and left £40 to each of the churches at Llanblethian and Cowbridge to be spent on the fabric of the buildings.

Subsequent occupants were Sarah Rogers, the widow of an ironmonger and stationer who had lived at 35 High Street, with her two children in 1891; Evan Hopkins, the monumental mason whose workshop and yard was over the then river bridge - where Penny Lane is today; and the Misses Llewellyn in 1923 after they had moved from Heath House. It is still a private house today.

44 Eastgate - The Ancient Druid

This grade II listed building is of medieval origin but the present structure is largely of 18th century date. It has a surviving medieval doorway and the rendered three-bay front has chamfered quoins, and moulded architraves to the upper floor windows with a square wooden panel with a relief carving of a heraldic griffin or dragon over all window heads.

In 1766, this was the house of Catherine Williams. In 1785 Oliver Richards, yeoman, leased the house to Elizabeth Sands of Llandough and the Sands family retained its connection with the property until 1844, when it was sold to Martha Ballard. By 1851 it was a beer house with David Williams as publican and was known as the *Ancient Druid*. In 1861 William Miles, a mason and victualler, was in occupation. He was followed by Joseph May who owned the property for eight years but who remained as licensee until the 1880s. In 1881, he was living here with his widowed daughter and six grandchildren. In 1891 the house was occupied by Richard Morgan, a hay merchant, and by 1920 Wybert Thomas was using the premises as an office for his building company.

The Ancient Druid is alleged to be the oldest private house in Cowbridge and it is claimed that it was once a rest stop for pilgrims en route to St David's.

8 Eastgate - St Crispin

St Crispin was constructed in 1894 by W A James, builder, of Stafford House, Cowbridge. The owner was Morgan Morgan who kept the *Commercial Inn*; he had the house constructed on the site of a previous dwelling which he had bought from Nathaniel Bird the ironmonger. In 1843 that had been owned by James Bird and for some time was occupied by a master shoemaker, Evan Edwards, who had been born in Penllyn, and his family. The name of the new house was most appropriate as St Crispin is the patron saint of shoemakers.

Morgan's first tenant was Dr John Watkin Phillips who used a pony and trap when visiting patients. Behind the premises are a stable, loft and coach house (later used for photographic processing when Forest Burton the photographer lived here). At the end of the 19th century dwelling houses in Cowbridge had no running water, and so rainwater was stored in large underground cisterns which had to be white-washed annually. At St Crispin, under the kitchen floor, a 16-foot-deep cistern still exists.

In 1912 the house was occupied by Edward Williams, stationmaster, followed by Wybert Thomas, builder, in 1914. Wybert was a popular, flamboyant character who was a councillor and twice mayor of the town. He was the grandfather of the Thomas brothers, the present funeral directors of Cowbridge. Wybert's third wife, Sarah, purchased St Crispin in 1920; it passed to Henry Gibbs, the baker of Town Hall Square, in 1937 and is still a private house today.

25 to 29 Eastgate

These modest terraced properties are included to show that they too have a varied history, and were never built as one unit. On this site in the mid 18th century, there were two houses and a smithy, all owned by Jenkin Williams, a wealthy Cowbridge landowner. In 1769/70 his widow and two daughters (one then living in New York) sold the properties to the tenants - to David Abraham the blacksmith and to Thomas Rhys.

The westernmost properties remained in the ownership of the Abrahams - grandfather, father and son, all blacksmiths - until 1852, and then, even though they were bought by Robert Stibbs the baker, the forge remained in operation under Thomas Morgan for some time. By 1874, however, it was 'formerly a smith's forge, now a stable' and the house (where No 29 is today) was occupied by Thomas Jenkins, brewer's drayman, and Joseph Hall, commission agent and hay factor who sold hay from Vale of Glamorgan farms to collieries for the use of pit ponies.

By 1876, new houses had been built on the site of both the stable (No 27) and of Thomas Rhys' house (No 25) by the new owner, John Evans, a carpenter from Llysworney. At the turn of the century, Jenkin Evans, also a carpenter, lived in No 25 and Richard Thomas, a grocer, in No 27. The old house of Jenkins and Hall had become 'ruinous' and was rebuilt early in the 20th century.

No 27 (Wadhams the grocers from 1922 to 1996) remains a grocery store, Newschase Minimarket, while the adjoining properties are private houses.

69 Eastgate – Kumalo House

A grade II listed building, this is a late 17th to early 18th century house, with an interesting inwardly canted window on the ground floor, large ceiling beams and a massive chimney breast. By 1773 it belonged to Robert Taynton, having been bequeathed to him by Nathaniel Taynton, his father, when it was described as 'lately purchased from Thomas Wyndham'. The occupier in 1778 was John Evan, described as a shoe-maker and shopkeeper – but the house is also reputed to have been a coffee tavern in the 18th century.

It passed into the ownership of the Lewis family (the Revd John, a fellow of Jesus College, Oxford, followed by Richard and later Catherine) in the early years of the 19th century. By 1843, William Williams owned and occupied the house, and he was followed by the Revd John Evans, the Baptist minister, in 1851. Ten years later, Jane Barnes, a schoolmistress born in Llysworney, lived in the house with a governess, a servant and ten girl boarders: thus it is likely to have been a school for a short time. Edward Bates, a doctor and surgeon born in St Brides, lived here (or next door at No 67) for about 20 years, to be followed by Samuel Hayter, the Cowbridge photographer, in 1891.

Lewises reappeared in the building as shopkeepers in 1912. William Henry Lewis kept a general store, and Miss Winifred Arnott a needlework shop in the same building in the 1920s. It has now reverted to a private residence, the name 'Kumalo' relating to African interests of the present occupier.

71 Eastgate

This grade II listed building is probably a late 16th to early 17th century property. The modern shop front masks an interesting interior, especially on the first floor, where there is a massive fireplace lintel, and also fragments of 17th century wall paint. The rear extensions to the building were probably separate dwellings in the 19th century.

Despite the age of the building, we can so far only trace occupants back to 1800, when Thomas Jenkins was both owner and occupier, paying a very modest 2/- rate of land tax. By 1821 this was one of a number of buildings owned by Isaiah Verity. Edward Morgan, a master shoemaker, born in Cowbridge lived here in the 1840s and 50s, and was followed by Eliza Edwards, a fruiterer, in 1861. It is probable that the property was then occupied by Richard Morris, a 80-year-old confectioner from St Mary Church. His wife Ann, 26 years his junior, had succeeded him by 1881, and by 1891 was in business as a grocer. Throughout that century separate families lived in the rear rooms, sometimes described as 'lodgers' but having no apparent family or trade connections with the main occupants.

Stanton's fish and fruit shop in 1912 was soon succeeded by Alice Chissell's shop. More recently it has been a hairdresser's - Olwen Muir's, Theresa's and currently Anthony Haircare. There is residential accommodation above.

73 Eastgate

This grade II listed building is considered by the Royal Commission on Historical Monuments to have been originally part of one property with No 71. The 16th century stone doorway to No 71 is best seen from inside the shop at No 73, and the first floor above the shop has infilled windows which can only be seen from inside the loft above the shop. At the rear is a range of buildings which once housed a number of families - in Bethuel's Court.

Another of Isaiah Verity's properties, it was occupied from the date of the tithe map (1843) for about 20 years by a tailor journeyman from Cardigan, John James and his wife Sarah. By 1871 Patrick Fitzgerald from Ireland, a china dealer, had moved here from Cardiff with his wife, four children and mother-in-law. By 1881 Thomas Tucker from Martock in Somerset was selling china here, with his wife and four children. Parish records show that seven additional Tucker children died in infancy between 1883 and 1900. Thomas Tucker stayed in 73 Eastgate until the turn of the century, when a number of photographs show his new shop at the side of what would be Bridge Garage today. One of the children, Henry, remained in No 73, running it as a fish and fruit shop in 1912.

After this, some Cowbridge folk still remember 'Bopa Cato', Catherine Jenkins, who sold sweets and lemonade - a ha'penny for a glass of pop! For some time the shop has been an ironmongers and builder's merchants - JBs.

77 Eastgate - Lynthurst

Like a number of properties belonging to the Veritys in the 1830s and 1840s, this house passed to D J Harmer of Bridgend; in 1864 it was sold to Julius Simonnet, the French master of the Grammar School, who lived in Dynevor Cottage. He continued the lease to David Rees, a draper, who had been using the property in conjunction with the house next door since about 1850. David Rees had been born in Margam, but had established himself in Cowbridge by the time he was 26, in 1843. In 1851 he was employing three others; ten years later, he called himself a master draper and employed eight. By then he had seven children - and also employed three servants.

Rees was still here in 1881, with his wife as a linen draper, and three of his adult children as assistants - but in 1883 Howell and Co took over the business as a 'first class millinery, dressmaker and general drapery department'. They left fairly quickly, however, and in 1886 the house was sold to W T Gwyn the solicitor.

There are still two doorways which mark the position of the former interconnecting passages between the two properties; these were blocked up and the two premises made completely separate in the early years of the 20th century. The firm of Gwyn and Gwyn was based here for a few years, but it remained the home of W T Gwyn. After the second world war, one of the doctor's surgeries of the town, first of Dr Miller and then of Dr Naysmith, was housed here. It is now a private residence.

79 Eastgate

For much of the 18th century, this was the home of the Miles family; the land tax assessment of 5/- in 1773 to the Revd William Miles, vicar of Llanblethian, suggests that it was a substantial property. By 1800, owner-ship had passed to Isaiah Verity, who also owned the houses to the east.

From 1850 to about 1883 this building and No 77 formed one unit, containing a house and draper's shop occupied by the Rees family.

Almost as soon as W T Gwyn moved into the house next door in 1886, this property was conveyed to Charles Jackson Gwyn, WT's brother. It was used, however, as a grocer's shop - in 1887 it was described as 'about to be occupied by John and William Pickard, grocers'. It was John Pickard who lived here, with his wife, two sons and a domestic servant, until his death in 1912. He was the son of Richard Pickard who kept a grocer's shop at 40/42 High Street. In 1881, John was described as a cabinet maker, but perhaps his marriage to a neighbour, Augusta Lewis, directed him to a more secure occupation. Mrs Pickard continued the business after John's death, but in 1919 the property was conveyed to the Cowbridge RDC for use as offices.

The building remains in the use of the Vale of Glamorgan Council, and includes a tourist information office; the Citizens Advice Bureau has an office at the back of the building.

81 and 83 Eastgate

This pair of well-proportioned early 20th century houses was built by David Brown the printer (hence the name Caxton House for one), on the site of one earlier larger house. The other name, Plas Hen, was that of the earlier building.

In the 18th century, however, there were probably two buildings here. The western side (No 83) originally belonged to the Carnes, and No 81 to the Deere family. This latter house had been in 1701 occupied by the Freames, aldermen of Cowbridge. David Morgan, a baker, lived in the Carne house in 1748, but both houses had been taken over by Mrs Alice Gibbon by 1785. Ownership by the Thomas Williamses, father and son, probably saw the rebuilding around 1800 of a house which was among the most valuable in Cowbridge.

By 1843, the owner was W Samuel, but it was occupied by the Savours family, landed proprietors, until after 1861. In 1851 Alice Savours, from Middlesex, lived here with her sister, a companion and three servants - a fairly leisured life! Eleanor, the sister, is mentioned on the benefactions board at Holy Cross church: she left £200 to be invested for the benefit of the poor of the parish.

Thomas Llewellyn, described as a banker, landed proprietor, town magistrate, alderman and retired corn merchant, then lived here when the house was owned by John Samuel Gibbon. Llewellyn was succeeded by Alice Payne, schoolmistress (and two schoolgirl boarders) for a short time before David Brown bought the house in 1906. Maud Gunter, the local historian, lived in Plas Hen for a time in the 1920s; both houses are still private residences.

85 and 87 Eastgate

These two properties have the appearance of being one house, and this was the case in the 18th and the first half of the 19th centuries. With a land tax assessment of 6/-, it was a sizeable and valuable building.

Ownership by James Reynolds by 1843, however, saw it divided into two properties. No 87 was occupied by shoe shop owners for about 100 years - the Mustoes, who had come from Bristol, from 1843 to 1871, and Catherine David and her 'boot warehouse' from 1891 to 1920 (and after that, William Llewellyn from 1923 to 1932).

No 85 was essentially residential throughout the 19th century, housing the family of Daniel Edwards, surgeon, for over 20 years. The 20th century saw its use as a cafe (the Gypsy Tea rooms) - note the Cyclists Touring Club badge on the wall - and above, a maternity home, run by Miss Helen Rymer, where some of Cowbridge's illustrious citizens were born.

More recent occupiers include 'Bob Morgan the Mace', a grocery store, Davies and Llewellyn Fine Art, and Eastgate Antiques. The present occupants are Beauty Within and '87 Eastgate', a dress shop.

89 Eastgate

Belonging in 1690 to Pierce Deere, a prosperous farmer of Llanquian Isaf in Aberthin, this house was one of the properties which passed via his heir Pierce Cornish to John Wilson, a saddler, who was declared bankrupt in 1768. It was then bought, with other properties, by Benjamin Thomas, a wealthy Cowbridge shopkeeper and maltster, as 'a messuage or cottage and garden in the possession of George Thomas'. In fact it seems to have been very much an 'investment property' for some time. Thomas, then his widow, had a number of tenants, as did Isaiah Verity, the builder of Cowbridge's new Town Hall, for the first 30 years of the 19th century, and then James Reynolds, draper and auctioneer, for the next 30 years.

John Jones, a draper and tailor, lived here in the 1850s, followed by the Revd John Thomas. Edmund Davies, a linen draper, owned and occupied the building for over 20 years, succeeded by John Williams the draper who also owned the house next door (No 91).

The house was rebuilt during the ownership of John Williams in a pleasant late Victorian style with some nice details of stonework and woodwork. Known as London House, it transferred to the Jacob family in 1935. Since 1964, the ground floor has been used as an optician's premises (currently David Fine), with office and residential use above.

91 Eastgate

A record as early as 1690 suggests that this property, on the then eastern bank of the River Thaw, on half a burgage plot, was leased by a glover, John Thomas, to his niece Mary Gibbon. The Edmondes family of Old Hall owned the property standing here through much of the 18th and early 19th centuries, and for many of these years it was leased to Thomas Hopkins, and then to James Reynolds, a tailor, who bought this and adjoining houses around 1830.

For most of the 19th century it remained in the hands of tailors and linen drapers, often linked with the next-door house. John Jones, 'draper and tailor' was here in 1851, while John Williams ran his thriving drapery, tailoring and millinery business in this property from the end of the 19th century through to 1935. Along with No 89, it was known as London House and contained workshops upstairs as well as an 'emporium' of drapery. John Williams, a staunch nonconformist, operated a charitable scheme or club for people who had difficulty in affording garments. Fund-raising for the club included concerts held in St Hilary where Mr Williams originated.

The Jacobs family of drapers then took over, but during the second world war the building was used as a British Restaurant, feeding local children who were marched here in file every day from the junior school for their mid-day meal. The canteen at the rear is now derelict, but for many years the front part of the building has been Cowbridge's only betting shop - Jack Brown, bookmaker.